PROBSTHAIN'S ORIENTAL SERIES
VOL. XVIII

FOLKWAYS IN CHINA

FOLKWAYS IN CHINA

BY

LEWIS HODOUS
(Hartford Seminary Foundation)
HARTFORD, CONNECTICUT

ARTHUR PROBSTHAIN
(LATE PROBSTHAIN & CO.)
41 GREAT RUSSELL STREET, LONDON, W.C.
1929

STEPHEN AUSTIN AND SONS, LIMITED
PRINTERS, HERTFORD

PREFACE

THIS volume is the result of personal observation during a long residence in China. The gathering of the material took the writer on many a pleasant jaunt. While much of the work was done at Foochow other parts of China made substantial contributions. Some of the stories were picked up on a two hundred mile walk through Shansi. Other bits were collected in Hunan and Hupeh. A visit to Canton and Hongkong one New Year confirmed observations elsewhere. An overland journey from Amoy to Foochow and a thousand mile trip through western Fukien added to the store.

But quite as important as the material gathered on excursions were the contributions of many Chinese and residents in China from different lands. To these friends I acknowledge my debt not merely for the material obtained but for the pleasant memories of fellowship and interchange of ideas.

Observation and conversation were supplemented by a wide reading in Chinese sources. The local and provincial histories contain much interesting material on the folkways. Then there are works on local customs and usages. The most ancient of these is found in the Book of Rites. The monographs in other languages were found quite helpful, especially the work of J. J. M. de Groot, Doolittle, Grube, and Chavannes.

The illustrations were selected from a large number collected during several years. Some of them are quite unique and were obtained after long diplomatic negotiations. At present it is quite easy to obtain photographs in China, but some years ago it was more dangerous than taking snapshots of Japanese fortifications.

It is hoped that this work will make a contribution to the understanding of the Chinese who live and toil on the soil.

LEWIS HODOUS.

HARTFORD, CONN.

CONTENTS

CHAPTER		PAGE
I.	Preparation for the New Year	1
II.	The New Year	10
III.	The Reception of Spring	19
IV.	The Pearly Emperor	26
V.	The Lantern Festival	41
VI.	The Story Hour	48
VII.	The Tutelary Gods of the Ground and Grain	58
VIII.	The Filial Porridge	66
IX.	The Goddess of Mercy	68
X.	The God of Literature	75
XI.	K'uei Hsin	78
XII.	Lü Tung Pin	81
XIII.	The Feast of Cold Food	86
XIV.	The Ch'ing Ming	92
XV.	Ploughing the Field	94
XVI.	The Great Year	97
XVII.	The Shepherd's Purse	100
XVIII.	Empire and Religion	103
XIX.	T'ai Shan	113
XX.	The Inauguration of Summer	123
XXI.	The Dragon Boat Festival	126
XXII.	The Dragon Boat Races	132
XXIII.	The Dragon	139
XXIV.	Mother Earth	146
XXV.	The Summer Solstice	152
XXVI.	The Ruler of Earth	158

CONTENTS

CHAPTER		PAGE
XXVII.	The God of War	164
XXVIII.	The Weaver and the Herdsman	175
XXIX.	The Harvest Festival	179
XXX.	Kite Flying	190
XXXI.	The City Guardian	193
XXXII.	The Winter Solstice	198
XXXIII.	The Eight Spirits	202
XXXIV.	The Hunters' Festival	203
XXXV.	Cleansing Processions	205
XXXVI.	The God of the Hearth	214
XXXVII.	The Sacrifice to Heaven during the Manchu Dynasty	220
	List of Works consulted	237
	List of Chinese Names	242
	Index	245

ILLUSTRATIONS

	PAGE
Temple where the Emperor prayed for a good year	10
An Offering to Buddha	16
Contest with Lions	42
Goddess of Mercy, Kuanyin	68
The Laughing Buddha	72
Old Examination Halls at Nanking	76
Ploughing in South China	94
An Offering to Jupiter	98
Court of T'ai Shan in Hades	114
Dragon Boats	132
Shrine to General Ward at Sunkiang	158
Solving the Eternal Problem	186
Offering for Long Life	194
Wang T'ien Kung, a Demon Expeller	200
A Taoist Swallowing a Sword	206
Sending off the Demons of Disease	210
The Kitchen God	214
The Altar of Heaven	220

CHAPTER I

THE PREPARATION FOR THE NEW YEAR

According to a modern Chinese philosopher the Indian studied nature in order to be able to escape it, the West investigated nature in order to control it, while the Chinese studied nature in order to adapt themselves to her ways. The folkways are the methods by which the Chinese have harmonized their life with the changing moods of nature.

The Chinese term for festival means a joint or node which marks the critical time in the breathing of nature when it passes from one mood to another. During this transition man should so conduct his life that he will bring the process to completion. From the emotional responses on the part of social groups to adapt themselves to the breathings of nature have arisen the folkways.

The most important of these nodes in the breathing of nature is the New Year. Preparation for this transition begins many days before. Sometime during the twelfth month the spacious reception room is washed. The large doors are taken from their sockets and scrubbed with sand. The old mottoes on the posts and doors are scraped off and new ones pasted in their place. These mottoes reflect the ideals of the family. In business houses they invite prosperity, in official houses they express the hope for official position and honour. In all families they exalt the virtues of filial piety and reverence. In recent years they have expressed the longing for an established government, a prosperous China and a peaceful world. Over the lintel of the door appear such sentiments as " May we receive the hundred blessings of Heaven " or " May Heaven send down the five blessings". These consist of wealth, posterity, longevity, absence of pain and of sickness. Another more idealistic list contains long life, riches, peace, love of virtue and a good end crowning life. These mottoes not only express pious longings as do mottoes in our homes, but the characters are regarded as possessing the magic power to attract the blessings which they symbolize.

Many households still place on the outside door the pictures of Shen Tu and Yü Lei, two brothers who ruled the spirits of Tu Shuo mountain in the north-eastern part of our world. They caught the evil spirits and bound them with sedge-grass rope and gave them to the tigers to eat. This is a relic of the old myth of the sun as the great destroyer of darkness and the spectres associated with it. Here also is the nucleus of the future idea of Hades.

On this mountain grew a peach-tree whose branches spread over three thousand *li* and whose fruit conferred longevity and immortality, and so the people still paste the pictures of these two heroes and place a peach charm over the door. The red paper on the posts and doors derives its power from the red peach and the peach its power from the sun.

During the last month of the year every family lays in a supply of provisions to carry them over the New Year. Ducks and chickens and pork, supplies of rice and other grains, as well as fuel are stored away. Little business is done during the first few days of the New Year, and hence this precaution is quite necessary.

The New Year is the great settling day for outstanding accounts. There are other days for settlement such as the fifth day of the fifth month and the fifteenth of the eighth month, but this is the most important one. In case the debtor fails to pay, he not only is made miserable, but will find it difficult to obtain credit during the coming year. The merchants sell their goods at reduced prices in order to attract ready cash. The large pawnshops are crowded with people anxious to convert things into cash. Lands, houses, personal property, and even children are sold in order to meet the demands of creditors. Business is brisk and the time is opportune to make purchases of all kinds if one has ready money. The debtor in order to escape his creditor attends theatricals. The creditors also are led to the same place by another instinct and violent scenes not a part of the play are enacted among the audience. Even church services to watch for the New Year have been advocated, but it should be said to the credit of the Christians that such services have never been popular. The creditor pursues his quarry through the night and into the New Year. He is permitted to continue his search after daybreak as long as one candle burns in his lantern. The creditors carry several candles which they insert clandestinely and continue the search long after the New Year sun has dawned. Western business methods are changing the old ways, but this habit of demanding settlement persists.

The end of the year is not only the time for the settlement of mundane accounts, but also for the thank-offerings to the gods for past favours and for prayer for future blessing. The gift to the gods is the means of connecting the worshipper with the divine power and is especially appropriate at this time. The household gods common to all parts of China are the kitchen god, the god of wealth, and Kuanyin, the goddess of mercy. Besides these each locality has deities which are placed in the family pantheon. These are all remembered toward the end of the year with incense, candles, and food.

There is also an offering made to the spirit ruling the material heaven and the spirit of earth and all the gods who have blessed the family during the year. This offering is very old. It is noted in the Li Chi which was collected before the Christian era and which gives the following directions for the twelfth month: "All the people of the nine provinces of the empire should according to their strength make offerings and sacrifices to Shangti of August Heaven, to the tutelary gods of the ground and grain, to the ancestral temple, to the gods of the mountains, to forests, and to famous streams."

This offering is made in the main reception room facing the court. On a table are placed an incense burner, candles, vases with flowers, ten bowls of different kinds of meat, ten cups of wine and ten bowls of vegetables. Ten is the perfect number and hence is significant in this ceremony. In vegetarian households the offering contains no meat. When all is ready the head of the house lights three sticks of incense and raising them reverently to his forehead in both hands places them in the incense burner. Then he kneels before the table three times and at each kneeling bows thrice with his head touching the ground. In some families a brief prayer of thanksgiving is uttered to Heaven for the blessings of the year. In others the ceremony is performed in silence while the members of the family stand about. The worship is concluded with the burning of idol paper money in an earthern vessel and a fusillade of fire-crackers.

Not only do the Chinese give presents to the gods, but they remember each other. The husband gives presents to the parents of his wife and they remember their married daughters with appropriate gifts. The names of the presents or the characters placed upon them suggest prosperity, blessing, progeny, and other desirable things. A popular present is the New Year's cake, a round dark brown soggy piece of pastry three inches thick and from eight to fifteen inches in diameter, made of rice flour, brown sugar, peanuts, and dates. Its name sounds the same as the word for "high" and so the gift of the cake conveys the wish for a prosperous year. Goat's or pig's feet are also a favourite present in certain parts of China. Other presents symbolize the great wants of the Chinese people, longevity, progeny, health, wealth, and official honours.

In certain parts of China on the last evening of the year each family burns before the door of the house a small pile of wood. Some throw their old bamboo lanterns, or some other object into the flames and as the flames blaze up they sprinkle salt over them, which gives forth a crackling sound. The children stand about with masks covering their faces to prevent them from catching smallpox.

The explanation in Foochow of this custom is that many years ago there lived a man, Dang Dong by name, who was cordially hated by some of his neighbours. These brought a coffin to his house on the last day of the year in order to bring calamity upon him. He, nothing daunted, broke the coffin up and burned it in the fire. As the fire crackled he sang:—

> "Dang Dong the coffin burned
> And dire calamity to good luck turned."

The custom is of course much older than this story and is really a way of leaving the past behind not merely by turning a new leaf, but by burning the old one. People also jump over the fire and thus rid themselves of the bad influences which might otherwise follow them into the New Year. We find traces of similar customs in other lands. In Mexico the Indians used to burn part of their old utensils in order to leave the old behind them.

The letting off of fire-crackers accompanies every festival and popular offering. Originally the people put bamboo in the fire which exploded with a loud noise when the liquid within the sections expanded. The earliest notice of this is in the sixth century of our era, but undoubtedly the bamboo was employed for the purpose of frightening demons much earlier. The fire-crackers at present are made in Hunan and Kiangsi, but especially in the district of Yimpu in Kwangtung. In recent years alum has been used to neutralize the smoke in them. The object of the fire-cracker is to frighten away the demons who may be prowling about when an offering is made. The last night of the year resounds with the fusillade of bunches of fire-crackers punctuated frequently by the explosion of giant crackers.

It is often said that the Chinese employed gunpowder earlier than the West, but that they did so against the demons.

We have records, however, of the use of powder in bombs in the siege of cities. The powder was put into an iron shell, or when that was lacking, into a porcelain receptacle which was hurled into the camp of the enemy. The projective power of powder was an invention of the West.

On the last evening of the old year an offering is made to the wandering spirits who have met a tragic death away from home and who have no one to look after their needs. A platter with a bowl of vegetable soup, a bowl of rice and one of dumplings is placed on the ground before the house. Two candles and three sticks of incense are placed before it. A quantity of paper with pictures of warm clothing is burned. The rice and dumplings are picked up by a passing beggar. The head of the house turns toward the cheery home conscious of having done a meritorious act and this is a protection against some of the ills of this season.

When the shops are shut up for the night a few sheets of idol money are fastened between the boards which, in many parts of China, are used to close the front of the shop. The following year when the shop is opened for business the paper is burned before the door as an offering to the guardian spirit of the door.

New Year is a time of reunion. It is the one time when everyone comes back to the parental roof. It is a reunion not only with the living, but with the dead who share in the joy and the prosperity of the family. The feast is spread first before the ancestral tablets either in the main reception room of the house, or in the room behind where the cabinet with the ancestral tablets is kept. There arranged in order are the tablets of father and mother and of ancestors five generations back. On the centre of the table is a large incense burner with rising clouds of smoke, vases with flowers, immense spluttering red candles, ten bowls of hot food with spoons and chopsticks beside them and ten small cups of steaming wine. Everything is served as though the ancestors were actually present.

In the Chinese language the same sound may mean various things. The food presented has this symbolic meaning. The word for duck also means to repress and so this offering contains a prayer that evil influences may be suppressed. The sound for chicken in certain parts of China also means to bind and so the bowl with the chicken utters the prayer that the family may be kept in life united. The long strings of vermicelli convey the wish for long life. The sound for oysters suggests a numerous progeny. The New Year's cake symbolizes prosperity.

When all is ready the members of the family attired in holiday garb gather together. The head of the family lighting three sticks of incense, holds them in both hands as high as his forehead and places them in the incense burner before the tablets. Then he kneels thrice and at each kneeling bows thrice. The other members follow according to their rank. Idol paper is burned and the usual crackers are let off.

During the evening the children and the servants are given a little money wrapped in red paper for good luck. When the ancestors have partaken of the etherial essence the members of the household consume the material part. They spend the whole night in feasting, drinking large quantities of steaming red wine, munching mellon seeds and playing fingers.

Cares are left behind with the old year. The individual is permeated by a social impulse. He feels the power of the presence of his ancestors. His joy reinforced by the presence of the members of the family and the ancestors follows him into the New Year.

CHAPTER II
THE NEW YEAR

The Chinese government has adopted the Western calendar, but the people still follow the old style according to which the year begins with the first new moon after the sun has left the sign of Capricorn. This brings the first day of the year between 21st January and 19th February. There are twelve months in the year, being designated as the first, second, etc. Each month begins with the new moon and the fifteenth day of the month corresponds to the full moon. The months have twenty-nine and thirty days. Inasmuch as the lunar year is shorter than the solar year the days which gradually accumulate are put into an intercalary month which is announced beforehand in the almanac. The Chinese have really a combination of the solar and the lunar year which has certain advantages. The first three months are spring, the second three summer, and the third autumn, and the fourth winter. The vernal equinox occurs in the second month of spring and the autumnal equinox in the second month of autumn. The solstices come in the second month of summer and winter.

The first day of the year is regarded not only as the beginning of the year, but as the root out of which the day, the month, and the year and the events of the future grow. Accordingly what one does and what happens on the first day has a great influence upon the life of the whole year. The Chinese take every precaution to begin the year right.

The transition from the old year to the new is made by an

TEMPLE WHERE THE EMPEROR PRAYED FOR A GOOD YEAR, PEKING.

offering to Heaven and Earth who are regarded as the father and mother of the people. While this custom is general throughout China, the form varies in different parts. The following has been observed in Foochow. Just before dawn of the New Year the main reception room of the house is swept and the offering to Heaven and Earth is spread upon a table. In the centre of the table is placed a red lacquered bucket with boiled rice and a ladle. In the rice are stuck ten pairs of red chopsticks. On one pair is hung the almanac for the year. On the rice are arranged a mandarin orange, five different kinds of seeds and fruits such as melon seeds, dates, peanuts, dried persimmons and filberts. In the rice is also a spray of artificial flowers representing the four seasons with an image of a little boy in one of the flowers. The orchid represents spring, the lotus summer, the olea fragrans autumn, and the flowering almond winter. There are also two roots of garlic tied with a red band, a species of green with a red root and two twigs of juniper. On the top of the chopsticks is an eight-sided drumlike affair made of gilded paper ingots representing money.

On the table are arranged an incense burner, two candles, two vases with flowers and a large circular platter divided into compartments in which are oranges, dates, melon seeds, candies, and other sweetmeats. There are also ten cups with tea leaves only. At the side of the table is an urn for burning idol paper.

Besides this offering in the main reception room incense and candles are lighted before the ancestral tablets and the household gods.

When all is ready just before dawn the head of the house

lights three sticks of incense, or one large stick, holds them in both hands as high as the forehead and places them in the incense burner. Then he kneels and bows, or just bows his head thrice. Idol paper is burned and fire-crackers are let off. The members of the family and servants stand quietly around the worshipper. In some families a vocal prayer is uttered, but usually the ceremony is conducted in silence. In fact, words are superfluous on this occasion because the offering symbolizes eloquently the prayers of the family group. The rice and the ladle are a prayer for plenty of food. The ten chopsticks, ten being a complete number and the sound for chopsticks also meaning to be present, express the prayer that the family circle may be kept intact. The orange by its red colour and by the sound of its name utters the prayer for good luck. The seeds and flowers indicate a call for children. The sound for juniper is the same as that for honour and its evergreen foliage stands for longevity. The almanac with the stamp of the government upon it is a powerful resister of evil and demons. The imitation ingots call aloud for wealth.

This simple ceremony, as ancient as the Chinese race, varying in detail in different parts of China, symbolizes the wants of the people, namely food, offspring, official honour, long life, wealth, and victory over demon powers. It is offered by scholar and peasant in palace and hovel. It represents more than a prayer for blessings. It expresses an attitude toward the universe and toward life. Dependence, reverence, submissive obedience, and the subordination of the individual to the group and the group to Heaven—these are the fundamentals of Chinese culture.

After the offering to Heaven and Earth the head of the household offers incense before the household gods and the tablets of the ancestors. The other members of the family in order of seniority also bow and kneel before the ancestor tablets.

After the religious ceremonies all the members of the household gather in the reception hall and pay their respects to their elders. The grandparents and parents are seated at the end of the room, the place of honour. The uncles stand near by. The younger members of the family kneel and bow before their betters. After them the servants do the same. In some parts of China they offer a cup of wine to the parents.

On New Year's Day many people abstain from meat for the purpose of promoting long life. As a rule the people stay indoors in many of the villages, though in the cities it is nowadays customary to go out on the streets. In former days the first few days of the year were considered taboo and among the aboriginal tribes in Yünnan and Kweichow are still so considered. The shops are closed, however, and remain so for three to five days. In olden days some shops did not open until after the fifteenth of the month.

Great care is taken to say nothing, or do nothing on the first few days of the year which might bring bad luck. There is no scolding, no swearing. The mother wipes the mouths of the youngsters with a piece of rough paper to neutralize any naughty words. The house is not swept for several days for fear that prosperity may be swept out. No water is drawn, no fire is given to neighbours, and no money is spent.

The first day of the year is propitious for fortifying the body against disease for the whole year. Many people dope themselves with all sorts of concoctions which have nothing better to recommend them than hoary tradition and a nasty taste. Tea made from the kernel of peach-stones contains the essence of the five elements and so is good for the suppression of demons. The fumes of an evil-smelling weed burned over charcoal are supposed to drive away disease. Some put three times seven beans in the well to avert pestilence, while others throw in a little sulphur. An old practice is to hang a brick from an old tomb above the door as a preventive of sickness.

The old-fashioned physicians still recommend a regimen in harmony with the season. A bit of wisdom from the seventh century uttered by a man named Sun is still authoritative: "During the first month the kidneys become weak and the lungs deteriorate. Accordingly very little salty and sour food should be eaten, and more of pungent food should be consumed. The latter stimulates the kidneys, builds up the lungs, and quiets the stomach. Do not walk carelessly over ice. Do not become overheated. Rise early. Retire early and thus harmonize your body and vital spirits."

In explanation of the above it should be said that the kidneys belong to the element water which at this time of the year is being used by the element wood. By sympathetic action the kidneys become weak because they lack water. Salty and sour foods tend to diminish the water element and hence should be avoided. On the other hand, pungent foods belong to the element metal which produces water.

The weather on the first day of the year determines the condition of the crops, the prices of grain, and even gives warnings of rebellions and troubles of all kinds. An old authority from the sixth century says: "If on the first day of the first month there are yellow vapours in the four directions the year will be a bountiful one. If the vapours are distributed evenly in the four directions the harvest will be good. If blue clouds are mixed with yellow clouds there will be insects producing blight. Red vapours indicate a great drought, black clouds indicate great floods. If the vapours about the star Jupiter are blue the year will be good for the mulberry. Red vapours favour beans and yellow favour rice." Jupiter is the guardian deity of the year, and of destiny because it makes one revolution in twelve years.

The direction of the wind is also significant. If the wind comes from the south rice will be cheap; if from the north rice will be expensive.

The first day is favourable for assisting the processes of nature. In the country districts about Foochow on the first day of the year at the fifth watch when the cock crows, the mulberry, date, and other fruit trees are warmed up with a torch to prevent attacks from insects. The trunk of the tree is struck rapidly with the blade of an axe, or a knife for the purpose of stimulating the growth of fruit. The bark of the peach is scraped off with a sharp knife for the same reason.

When the shades of night settle over the first day and the stars glitter in the sky, incense is placed on the table with the offering to Heaven and Earth and in a censer hung before the reception hall, or in the side posts of the house and before household gods and the ancestors. Thus, with a sweet odour rising to Heaven the first day is ended as it began, with an expression of man's dependence on and loyalty to the eternal in his heart and in the universe.

The Second Day

On this day and the four following days the offering of incense is made in the morning and evening to Heaven and Earth, to the household gods and to the ancestors. The taboo is lifted and the streets are crowded with happy people in their best holiday attire. Some are on their way to make calls on friends. They greet each other with "Happy New Year", or "Congratulation". The merchants say: "May you prosper," and the answer comes: "May we prosper together." Others are on their way to the temple to pay their vows and to obtain the blessing of the gods for the year. Most are out in response to that primal instinct of men and women to see and to be seen.

Every home keeps open house for friends and relatives. The guest is offered mellon seeds, mandarin oranges, and sweets. The teacup and the friendly pipe are passed round. The children who call with their elders are given mandarin oranges for good luck.

The shops are closed, but the gambling stands are doing a flourishing business. Here and there behind closed doors is heard the clatter of dominoes, or the shuffling of cards.

The ricksha men, the sedan bearers, donkey boys, and boat-people charge double fares and seem never more obliging and happy.

The Third and Fourth Days

The third day continues the festivities of the second. On the fourth day the Chinese receive the household gods who at the end of the year have gone up to heaven to report to the Jade Emperor, Yü Huang Shang Ti. The rice in the

AN OFFERING TO BUDDHA.

lacquered bucket offered to Heaven and Earth is reboiled and the same articles are placed in it as before. An offering is spread before the household gods and the ancestors and the head of the household pays his respects before them in the manner already described.

On this day a large red sheet with pictures of three gods is pasted at the end of the reception room. In the centre is a portly smiling god called the " Heavenly Ruler who grants blessing ". On his left is a small figure with silver shoes or ingots representing the god of wealth. On the other side a divinity with a high forehead holding the peach of immortality represents old age, while the children by his side stand for joy and progeny. Near the centre figure is a tall, stern individual with battle-axes, the slayer of evil. Above all is the character for happiness. In one corner is the picture of a bat, the sound for which is the same as that for happiness. Thus the Chinese begin the year with their minds fixed upon the fundamentals of life, longevity, prosperity, progeny, joy, and blessing resulting from the favour of the higher powers. This for many families concludes the festivities of the New Year and marks the commencement of the serious business of life.

THE FIFTH DAY

On the fifth day the house is swept for the first time ; the sweepings are taken out to the dumpheap and a stone is brought back for good luck. The story is told of a merchant of the T'ang dynasty who purchased a slave girl. As long as she was in the house his business prospered. One day, on the thirtieth of the twelfth month, in a fit of anger, he beat her and she disappeared in a broom. From that day misfortunes came upon him and he died a ruined man. Nowadays the people do not sweep the house in the early days of the year for fear of casting out Yu Yuan, this slave girl, the goddess of the broom. In some parts of China the sweepings are thrown into a stream. So in one way or another good luck is preserved.

This day is also called rice day because the rice offered to Heaven is reboiled and eaten by the members of the family.

So the Chinese begin the New Year with the confidence and joy which comes from the blessing of the gods and the goodwill of their fellow-men.

CHAPTER III

THE RECEPTION OF SPRING

One of the joyful days of the year during the last dynasty was that on which the new spring was received in the eastern suburb of the city. The Chinese divide their year not only into four seasons, the eight seasons, and the twelve months, but they also have twenty-four solar periods or breaths. The first of these is called the commencement of spring, which begins when the sun is fifteen degrees in the constellation of Aquarius.

The ceremony of receiving the spring is a very ancient one. In the Li Chi, in the rescripts for the first month of the year, we read: "This is the month in which the reign of spring is inaugurated. Three days before the inauguration of spring, the chief secretary informs the son of Heaven of the fact, saying: 'On a certain day spring will commence. The great power of spring is manifested in the element wood (i.e. vegetation).' The son of Heaven thereupon practices abstinence. On the day when spring arrives, the son of Heaven conducts the three superior ministers of state, the nine secondary ministers of state, the princes and the grand prefects to meet the spring in the eastern suburb. Upon his return he distributes gifts in the court of the palace to the superior ministers, the secondary ministers, the princes and the grand prefects."

In China the reception of spring was a state ceremony, but it was perhaps the most popular state ceremony, for all the people entered very heartily into it. In Foochow on the day before the commencement of spring the marine inspector, the two magistrates, and their deputies attired in fur-lined garments, proceeded in open sedans to the yamen of the prefect. After a bountiful feast they started with their retinue toward the eastern suburb. The procession was headed by a band of musicians. There were the tablets with the titles and offices of the magistrates. There were one or more umbrellas with ten thousand names given to a popular official when he leaves his post. All official decorations were exhibited on this occasion which was made as magnificent as possible. Behind the open sedan chairs of the officials followed a long line of attendants each carrying a bouquet of artificial flowers belonging to the spring season. On this day the prefect had the right of way through the streets, and so the viceroy and the higher officials residing in Foochow made this their at-home day, in order to avoid the unpleasantness of yielding the right of way to an inferior official.

The procession filed through the crowded streets, through the east gate to a pavilion called the pavilion of the spring bull. Here on an altar stood the spring bull. His ribs were made of mulberry wood plastered over with clay and covered with coloured paper. Beside the bull was an image of the tutelary god of the current year, called T'ai Sui, the Great Year. In the monthly rescripts of the Li Chi he is called Kou Mang. The god is connected with the star Jupiter, whose revolution in twelve years gives it great power in the eyes of the Chinese over the years on earth and the events which happen in them. Before these two images was a table with candles, an incense burner, fruits, and cups of wine. In front of the table were mats for the officials. Only the civil officials took part in this ceremony. The prefect stood before the table, the others took places behind him. On each side a ceremonial usher directed the ceremony. When the ceremonial usher gave the order to kneel the officials all knelt and bowed three times. They arose. An attendant at the left of the prefect handed a cup to him, and then poured the wine into it. The official raised it three times up to his forehead and then gave it to the attendant. Then the prefect bowed three times, the others likewise bowed. Then the musicians formed into line, the music struck up. The clay bull and the image of T'ai Sui were carried on a float into the city, the officials bringing up the rear. As the bull passed through the streets the people threw salt and rice at it. This was said to avoid the noxious vapours called *sha ch'i*. This throwing of salt and rice may possibly correspond to the custom mentioned in the Li Chi. " The son of Heaven ordered the officers to perform the great ceremonies for the dissipation of pestilential vapours, to dismember the victims and to disperse them in the four directions, to take out the clay bull and thereby to escort the cold vapours."

When the procession arrived at the yamen of the prefect, the officials formed a circle about the bull and each one struck it with a varicoloured stick three times, breaking off pieces of clay. The sound for the character three also means to produce and hence is regarded as propitious. The bits of clay and other parts of the bull were picked up by the crowd and thrown to their pigs to stimulate their growth.

Besides this public ceremony there is a reception to spring in each household. A table with an incense burner, candles, flowers, and three cups of wine is placed in the main reception hall at the edge of the court. The head of the family lights three sticks of incense, raises them to his forehead, and then places them into the burner. Then he kneels and bows thrice. Fire-crackers are let off, idol paper is burned. Some families invite Taoist priests to recite incantations on this day.

On this day the children are not whipped, nor scolded. All unpleasant things are avoided, the nightsoil is not removed. All things with strong odours are avoided.

What is the significance of the bull and the image of T'ai Sui? They contained an epitome of the coming year. All the details of their anatomy were carefully fixed the year before in the sixth month by the Imperial Board of Astronomy in Peking. The bull was made after the winter solstice on the first day denoted by the cyclical character *shen*. The ribs were made of mulberry wood because this is one of the trees which bud very early and hence possess much of the *yang* principle. The clay was taken from before the temple of K'ai Ming Wang, who was at one time ruler in Fukien. The bull was 4 feet high, to represent the four seasons. He was 8 feet long, in imitation of the eight seasons into which the Chinese divide the year. The tail was 12 inches long, to represent the twelve months of the year.

Thus far the anatomy of the bull is readily understood. What follows is very simple if we once obtain the key. The Chinese have ten characters which are called stems, and twelve other characters which are called branches. The first stem character is placed before the first branch character, and the second stem character before the second branch character, and so on, until all the combinations have been made. They number sixty in all and are called the *chia tzu*, the cycle. The cyclical signs were early employed in numbering days. Probably during the Han dynasty the cycle was applied to the years. The twelve branches are employed as names of the twelve hours into which the Chinese day is divided. Now these stem characters and branch characters belong to one of the five elements, or primordial essences, water, fire, wood, metal, and earth. These primordial essences are attached to the five colours. Moreover, these essences either repress one another as water does fire, or they produce one another as water produces wood. Here, then, we have the simple principles of a profound science. In order to understand the application we must remember that a character is not a mere sign of an idea, but is the double of the object which it signifies. It has a very real power over the object.

The different parts of the bull's anatomy have various colours which are determined by the cyclical characters. For example, the cyclical characters for the year 1911 were *shen hai*. The head of the bull is determined by the first character *shen*, which belongs to metal. Since metal is white, the head of the bull in 1911 was white. The colour of the body is determined by the second character in the cycle, namely *hai*. Now *hai* belongs to water, and water is black and hence in 1911, the last celebration under the dynasty, the body of the bull was black.

Each important part of the bull's anatomy corresponds to the cyclical character of the day, or the branch character for the hour of the day at which the procession takes place. We can readily imagine the refinement to which this can be carried. Once grant the premises, the whole system is very logically developed.

The year may belong to the male principle, or it may belong to the female principle. In case the year belongs to the male principle, the mouth of the bull is open. If the year belongs to the female principle the mouth of the bull is closed. If the year belongs to the male principle the tail of the bull is on the left side, because the left side belongs to the male principle. The reason for this is that the male principle belongs to the east. The emperor sits facing the south or is supposed to sit that way. His left is toward the east, and hence the left belongs to the male principle.

As to the image of Kou Mang, the tutelary god of spring and of the year, there are definite regulations. The image is 3 ft. $6\frac{5}{10}$ in. high. If we remember that a Chinese foot has 10 inches, we shall see that his height represents the 365 days of the year. The whip in his hand, which is 24 inches long, represents the twenty-four seasons. The age of the image, the colour of his clothing, the colour of his belt, the position of his coiffure, the holding of his hand over his left ear, or his right ear, his shoes, his trousers, in short every detail of his image, is determined by the cyclical characters for the year, the day, the hour, and the elements and colours which correspond to them, and by the quality which the five elements possess of either repressing, or producing one another.

The nose of the bull has a ring of mulberry wood. In Kou Mang's hand is a whip. The rope may be made of flax, grass-cloth fibre, or silk according to the cyclical characters of the day. If the inauguration of spring takes place before the New Year, the tutelary god of the year stands in front of the bull.

If it takes place five or more days after the New Year, the image is behind the bull. If it takes place between these dates, the image stands at the side of the bull. This position of the tutelary god of the year tells the husbandman whether to begin planting early or late. If the image stands in front of the bull the planting will be early in the New Year. The popular view held that if the image had both hands over his ears there would be much thunder. If he held his hand only over one ear there would be less thunder.

It is unnecessary to go into further details. The bull and the image of the guardian deity of the year epitomized the great events in the year to be. The ceremony was not only symbolic of the sun's power to bring the blessings of the year. It was a method of inducing the sun to return and dispense his gifts to expectant men. It left behind it a confidence and hope that the spring thus well begun would issue forth into summer and be crowned with bountiful harvests in the autumn.

This ceremony, so simple and beautiful, connects the Chinese with Europe with its May Day and various other customs of ushering in the spring of the year.

CHAPTER IV

THE PEARLY EMPEROR

The Pearly Emperor embodies the highest popular conception of a supreme being among the Chinese. The emperors of China from ancient times have worshipped Shangti, the supreme ruler of Heaven. No one but the son of Heaven, the emperor, was worthy to make an offering to Shangti. It was natural, therefore, that alongside of Shangti, the supreme ruler of the state religion, there should grow up a conception of a supreme ruler in the popular religion. The supreme ruler in the religion of the people is called Yü Huang, the Pearly Emperor or the Jade Emperor. Yü means jade, and hence immaculate and pure. Huang is made up of two characters according to the Shuo Wen (A.D. 121). The upper one means nose. According to the Chinese the nose was the member first formed. The nose boy was the first-born son. The nose above the character for king means that he is the first king, the first-born king.

He is also called Yü Ti. Ti designates divine beings and emperors. Max Müller connects it with the Sanskrit *de-va*, the Greek *theos*, and the Latin *deus*. The Sanskrit root *div* signifies light.

The origin of the name Yü Huang may be traced to the Book of Changes, which says: "The diagram Ch'ien (a cabalistic character for heaven) is heaven, is round, is ruler, is father, is jade, is gold." The heaven is characterized by the term jade and also called ruler.

It is difficult to say when the term Pearly Emperor was

first applied to the supreme ruler of heaven in the popular religion. The So Shen Chi (fourth century A.D.) mentions T'ien Kung, lord of Heaven, who is probably the same as our Yü Huang. Several poets of the T'ang dynasty (618–905) have written about the Pearly Emperor. In the Yu Yang Tsa Tsu, written at the end of the eighth century, we find this story regarding the venerable old man of heaven who is the precursor of the Pearly Emperor. "The surname of the venerable old man of heaven is Chang, his name is Chien, he is styled T'su Ke. He was a man of Yu Yang (name of a district in the Chihli province). In his youth he was very self-willed. No rule could bind him, he feared nothing. He caught a white sparrow and loved it and nourished it. He had a dream that Liu the old man of heaven scolded him angrily. Every time that Liu desired to kill him, the white sparrow informed Chien. Chien planned many ways to avoid the old man Liu, and finally the latter was unable to harm him. Once the old man Liu made a visit to Chien. Chien acting as host prepared a bountiful repast. Then he secretly mounted the chariot of Liu and drove the white dragon. With the whip in his hand he ascended into heaven. The old man of heaven, Liu, mounted the remaining dragons and followed him, but could not catch up with him. When Chien came to the remote palace he changed all the officials and barred the northern gate. He gave the white sparrow the title of supreme high mandarin. He transformed the descendants of the white sparrow so that they were no longer born in the world, but in heaven. When the old man Liu lost his throne he wandered among the five mountains, bringing calamities upon men. Chien feared him and so made him prefect of T'ai Shan, the

Eastern mountain, and gave him charge of the records of life and death."

We shall see at least some resemblances in this story to the one below which is taken from the work Kao Shang Yü Huang Pen Hsing Chi Ching, a eulogy of the Pearly Emperor. It probably dates from the Sung dynasty, A.D. 960–1278.

"Formerly there was a country, Kuang Yen Miao Yüeh by name, the ruler of which was Ch'ing Te, pure virtue, whose queen was Pao Yüeh Kuang, Precious Moonlight. The king had no children. One day, because of this, he thought as follows : ' Now I am growing old, and have no crown prince. When I die to whom shall the gods of the ground and grain, the nine temples (i.e. the empire) be handed over ? ' When he had finished these thoughts, he issued an imperial order proclaiming to all Taoist priests in all the courts of the palace according to their rules and teaching to hang up their banners and put up their canopies, to purify themselves strictly of all impurities, to spread the offerings of food, to perform the Taoist ceremonies six times, and pray to all the saints for an heir to the throne.

" After they had done this for a half a year with unabated zeal, one night suddenly the empress, Pao Yüeh Kuang, had a dream. She saw the supreme and high Lao Tzu together with all the holiest saints, a company pure and immaculate, glittering with jade and gold. He drove the chariot of the five coloured dragons, with the glorious illustrious banner with plumes and the canopy shading the bright clouds. The supreme and high Lao Tzu sat quietly in his dragon chariot holding in his arms a babe, the minute pores of whose body emitted a hundred myriads of beams shining into all the courts of the palace producing a hundred beautiful colours. The streamers and flags preceded him waving in the air. Then the heart of the empress was filled with joy. Respectfully with obeisance she received him, kneeling a long time before Lao Tzu. She spoke to Lao Tzu as follows : ' Now the king has no heir. I desire that you give him this child to become the lord of the tutelary gods of the ground and grain. Prostrate I desire compassion and mercy. Have compassion and pity, hear and answer.' Then Lao Tzu answered the empress saying : " My special desire is to grant you this child.' Then the empress respectfully thanked Lao Tzu and received the child. When the empress had received it, she awakened from her dream, and noticed that she was pregnant. She carried the child one year. In the *ping wu* year, the first month, the ninth day at noon she gave birth to a son in the king's palace. When he was born his body like a precious luminous light filled the king's country. His colour and form were wonderfully beautiful. Those who beheld it did not weary of it. In his youth he was compassionate and merciful. When he grew up he was kindly and loving. In his country he dispensed the treasures of all the precious wealth to the needy and the poor, widower and widow, the orphan, the childless, to those who had no one to depend upon, to those without rice and vegetables, to those who were maimed, to all beings. He was loving, peaceful, and mild. Men sung of him as possessing the heavenly Tao. His influence extended to distant regions. All under heaven looked up to him and obeyed him. They responded to the love of the crown prince. The father heaped favours on him.

" After this suddenly the announcement was made that the

king died. The crown prince took up the reins of government. He bowed his head and remembered the lowly beings. He issued a proclamation to the high officials to the effect that their succession to the throne was in accordance with Heaven's laws. Then he abdicated the throne and practised abstinence as a hermit in the P'u Ming Hsiang Yen Shan, i.e. Universal Brightness Incense Majestic Mountain. His virtue completed, he became a god. When he had passed this kalpa or age, he passed through eight hundred other kalpas. He gave up his country for the sake of all the living beings. He cut off that which was dear to him in order to practise the doctrine. After this he passed through another eight hundred kalpas. He dispensed medicine, healed diseases, and saved all beings, causing them to be peaceful and happy. When these kalpas were ended he passed through another eight hundred kalpas, doing deeds of kindness everywhere. He explained many Taoist books, expounding the spiritual precepts. He spread abroad the orthodox influence. He spread abroad the powerful deeds of the gods. He assisted the country to save men from Hades to the world of men.

"After this he passed through another eight hundred kalpas. His body was destroyed; he died. Because he bore disgrace patiently, he gave up his blood and flesh. Thus he practised abstinence for three thousand two hundred kalpas. Then he became an immortal. His title was the Pure, Quiet, Endowed with Intelligence King (who in coming into the world is like the coming of his predecessors). He taught all Buddhas to know quickly the correct doctrine of Abhidharma Pitaka, i.e. the philosophical works of Buddhism, and gradually to enter the wonderful doctrine of abstract contemplation. After this manner he practised abstinence for a myriad kalpas, and then he became the Pearly Emperor."

This story resembles in many respects the stories of other countries. Ezekiel saw in his vision the women weeping for Tammuz, the Babylonian god of vegetation. Tammuz goes to the under-world in the autumn when vegetation begins to decay. Ishtar follows him and tries to bring him back. The weeping of the women corresponds to the Taoist ceremonies and prayers for an heir to the throne. Tammuz was taken over by the Greeks and called Adonis. The Eleusinian mysteries performed in the autumn when nature was dying and in the spring when nature was reborn are connected with similar cosmic facts.

In Egypt we find a parallel in Osiris. He showed men how to use wheat and barley, he made instruments of agriculture, gave laws, instituted marriage, organized society, and taught men how to worship the gods. When he has made the Nile valley happy he goes to spread his benefits to the rest of the world conquering nations with his music and his eloquence. During his absence his throne is taken by his brother Typhon, who finally kills Osiris. Then Isis resurrects him. The soul of Osiris was supposed to be in the bull Apis. This bull was the emblem of spring and in him the Egyptians worshipped rejuvenated nature.

The stories which we have thus related all elaborate those recurring and wonderful phenomena of nature, its decay and death after the summer solstice and the mourning over it by mankind, its resurrection in the spring and the blessing which it dispenses. The king, Ch'ing Te, of the Chinese story is the sun, the queen is the moon. The king has no heir. After the summer solstice vegetation decays, the world becomes barren and sad and lonely. The king orders the priests to perform their ceremonies for a half year, which is the length of time between the summer solstice and the winter solstice. The son who comes is the revivified nature of spring which dispenses blessings to all mankind. Then the son gives up his realm and practises abstinence. This is another way of saying that the young and joyful spring attains the limit of its power and then begins the decay and barrenness of the autumn.

As we have already noted, the Pearly Emperor was known in the T'ang dynasty by this name and probably for many centuries before the T'ang dynasty by the name T'ien Kung, the lord of heaven. The T'ang dynasty was greatly influenced by Taoism and it is highly probable that the conception of the Pearly Emperor was elaborated during this dynasty. During this dynasty a brisk trade was carried on between China and the West. The missionaries of Christianity as well as those representing Buddhism came to China. It was an era of religious ferment, and so the conception of the Pearly Emperor was probably developed at this time, though we have only a few verses of poetry to testify to its influence.

In the year A.D. 1012, in the reign of Chen Tsung of the Sung dynasty, the Pearly Emperor was taken into the state pantheon. In the year A.D. 1013, a large image was set up in the imperial palace. In the year A.D. 1014 the same emperor granted the Pearly Emperor the title " The Great Supreme, Opening Heaven, Holding the Tablet, Regulating the Calendar, Embracing the Truth, Embodying the Tao, the exalted, great Heavenly Emperor ". His queen was given the title of " The Great Holy Queen of the Profound Heaven ".

The Pearly Emperor is mentioned in the State ceremonial in the year A.D. 1017.

During the Ming dynasty the worship of the Pearly Emperor fell into disfavour. In the Ch'ing dynasty this worship was branded as heterodox. An instance is on record in Fukien where the local sub-director of studies tore down the temple of the Pearly Emperor and used the materials to repair the Confucian temple.

The Pearly Emperor's palace is located in the constellation about the north pole called Ta Wei. The empyrean region is the source of all the life and energy of nature, the seat of all the vitalizing power that works upon the inert mass of the earth. His place is the highest. There is no heaven above it. It is called the wonderful, azure, limpid palace, the fathomless purple gold palace, the immaculate jade palace of Ta Wei.

In his jade palace the Pearly Emperor sits facing the south. His image as represented in his temple is the embodiment of passivity, inaction, and austerity. In his hands he holds a jade tablet. A crown of precious stones with pendants adorns his head. A long dark beard covers his breast. He is arrayed in a magnificent robe with embroidered dragons. Behind him are two attendants with large fans. On either side with their jade tablets are two ministers. On one side is the motto: "Heaven and Earth have no private interests to serve," on the other side are the words: "The gods investigate secretly." Before him is a tablet with the words: "He is able to reveal the good and evil of the world and fix men's wealth and rank, poverty, and low estate." His temples are found in the provincial capitals and the large cities.

The Pearly Emperor is called the exalted Shangti of the

azure vault. In the Tung Shan Lu, a devotional book written during the Ch'ing dynasty, he is called "the unapproachable, the unexcelled holy one, the solitary, great, without limitation. His powerful example controls the ten regions". He is the lord of all the heavens, the king of all the saints.

His rule was conceived of in the same way as that of the reigning emperor of China. The five emperors, the large number of Buddhas and Boddhisattvas, the numerous gods, the kings of hell, the *shen* are all under his command. He issues proclamations and is memorialized. His earthly mouthpiece was the Taoist pope.

According to the popular conception he is especially concerned with meting out justice to men. This he does through the gods and spectres, and the machinery ordained for this purpose in Hades. In fact, it may be truly said that this is regarded as the chief function of the Pearly Emperor among the people.

A few quotations from the popular devotional books will make this very clear: "The difference between good and evil has been clear from of old. Those who have taken notice of this difference have been few. The results of men's actions and the rewards have been very clear. The perverse and the blinded are numerous. The sins committed in a previous existence are serious, their roots are deep. In the present life the individual suffers on account of them. The blessing of the future is dependent upon present good conduct. One should deliberate before trouble comes upon him. When a man comes up against the staring guards of the Buddhist temples, he becomes cautious and careful, but when he notices the drooping eyelashes of the Buddha he again revives licentious and heterodox thoughts. If he is urged to lay the foundation of a holy life, he retorts that his friend is speaking wide of the mark. If he is urged to fulfill the doctrine of love, he turns a deaf ear.

"Vainly he strives after the fame of a hero. Wantonly he wastes large sums. His heart purchases the ephemeral joys of the brothel. His whole house is left empty and barren. He had love for his fellows, but he lost it. People tried once to please him, but now they disregard him. When it comes to the worst his father and mother are cold and hungry and he does not care. His brothers are at enmity and he is not concerned. While his evil associates flatter him his home folks scold him. But he retorts : ' I am suffering the obloquy usually attached to perfection.'

"There are those with whom the case is still worse. They quarrel with their wives and are ready to stab their brother. Such a man gathers together his inheritance and regards his parents as a virulent tumour. He hoards wealth, becomes a covetous person, and a gourmand. He kills wantonly many animals, desiring to satisfy his lascivious and covetous passion. All who are like this and yet are greatly blessed in the present life, will bring punishment upon their sons and grandsons. Those who have little blessing have brought calamity upon themselves. Their pretentious mansion becomes an empty hillock in a twinkling of an eye. Their wasted soul is tortured in the wheel of transmigration by swords and knives. Their poor son is given a beggar's bowl. Those who know him point him out as the scion of a certain family. His daughter goes begging for food dependent upon the charity of others. Those who know her laughingly say: 'This is N. N.'s beautiful daughter.'

"The sins committed before the present existence were not atoned for after death. Every injury to others is punished. When we speak of it, it is sad indeed. When one thinks of it cold sweat comes out of the body. You people should turn your ten thousand actions to good. From this time you should be filial and sincere. Every thought should be sincere. From this time on you should exert yourself to the limit of your capacity and purpose. If you have a good mother she will know how to prohibit the killing of animals and releasing live animals. If you have a good friend he will know how to surpass your sins and urge you to be good. Retreat a step backward when people want to quarrel with you. Do not speak of the shortcomings of others. When you are injured frequently by others, this is like ginseng and medicinal herbs which nourish life. Give to those who have not. Do all things sincerely. Help one another in emergencies. Do all things with all your strength. If your own life is miserable, your children will make your house great and famous. If in your previous existence you were evil, then practise secret benevolence in this life. In that way you will pay the debts of sin. Your secret acts will be known to heaven and earth who will not permit Pestilence to touch you, but will fill your house with its blessed light. Return and urge the members of your family to improve their conduct. Write these words on the right of the place where you sit. Announce them to all your friends."

These devotional books give a large number of instances of exemplary conduct which was greatly rewarded.

Here is a sample from the Yü Li Ch'ao Chuan Shih. It

describes the ten courts of hell and their punishments as a warning to the world. It is also a revelation from the Pearly Emperor. My copy was published in A.D. 1809 and reprinted several times since that date.

"At Huchow (Chekiang) Tsai Pei-lan was filial and loyal. Though he lived frugally himself, he gladly gave to those in need. To the poor, troubled and sick people he dispensed medicine. If orphans, or widows borrowed money of him he did not charge interest. If he met a woman or child who lost any article and could not return because they feared their elders, he planned ways to reimburse their loss. He saw the Regulation of the Pearly Emperor and was able thereby to warn the people of the world. He contributed money, hunted up good books, copied and distributed them, thus exhorting the world. He enjoyed the good old age of eighty-four. He was translated without sickness. His neighbours saw immortals, male and female, leading him to the chariot. His great-grandson, Tsai Chie-chung, in the ninth year of K'ang Hsi (1670) obtained the highest Hanlin degree. His great-grandson in 1682 received the first Hanlin degree."

Another quotation from the Kao Shang Yü Huang Pen Hsing Ching will illustrate other aspects. "The Pearly Emperor is the lord of all heavens, the king of all the saints. Therefore anyone who happens to obtain this classic and devotedly practises and obeys it, will obtain the help of the five emperors. The Pearly Emperor will order and despatch the multitude of immortals, he will employ the divine rulers, he will move the *yin* and *yang* principles. The thousand spirits will look upward respectfully. The ten thousand gods will bow with fear, the hundred evil influences will flee away, and the hordes of demons will be bound.

"When this life is ended he will ascend to the southern palace and there receive his reward. He will ascend the pure abode with flying steps. He will roam about at ease. He will be for ever with the Tao. Again turning to the living beings in the world who hear this classic and whose heart looks upward with a longing desire, if in their house they select a clean and quiet place and draw the exalted image of the emperor, and day and night are devout, morning and evening are respectful; if they nourish him reverently with incense, flowers, candles, and fruit; praise his holy name, and with respect and propriety repeat the classic, such persons will receive thirty kinds of very wonderful rewards.

"All the immortals will praise and honour such a man; his ancestors will be born in heaven; calamities will not injure him, and wherever he goes he will have a clear road; he will not be robbed; his prayers will be answered; he will escape flood and fire; obstructions will melt away secretly; his dreams will be lucky; disease and sickness will not come nigh him; he will be wise and intelligent; men will delight to see him; he will have abundance of food and clothing; his sons and grandsons will have glory and honour; the six grades of relatives will enjoy his presence (father, son, and up to the fourth cousin); his household will be at peace; he will escape pestilence, war, and famine; if a woman, she will be able to become a man; his appearance will be dignified and impressive; he will be a great official; he will be the son of an emperor; spectres and gods will look up to him; his life will be on a lucky star; all the gods will help him; the nine generations will receive his protection (from great-great-grandfather to great-great-grandson); he will enjoy a long life in the world; he will love men; he will be trusted; he will have goodness; the lord of demons will receive and protect him; he will cross over the three boundaries (heaven, earth, man); in open day he will ascend to heaven."

These long quotations reveal more plainly than any elaboration could do the system at the head of which the Pearly Emperor stands. Its purpose is to destroy sin, to inculcate righteousness by means of the punishments in this life and in hell and by the rewards of this life and the promise of joy in the life beyond the grave. The system strengthens the ideals of the Chinese taught in the classics, wrought out in the ferment of daily existence and received from other systems of religion, but regarded as native by the Chinese. The Pearly Emperor, to be understood, must be viewed as the head of this great system which has been promoting righteousness in China.

The birthday of the Pearly Emperor comes usually on the ninth day of the first month. The odd numbers belong to the *yang*. Number one is regarded as the beginning of the male principle and nine is looked upon as its completion. Either the first or the ninth day is appropriate for the celebration.

The celebration of the birthday is simple and impressive. Every household at daylight on the ninth day of the first month places on a table in the main reception room at the edge of the open court where it is exposed to the sky a brazier for incense, two candlesticks with red candles, and two vases of flowers. There are three small cups with dry tea leaves in the bottom, but no water. A large plate with vermicelli, whose long strings suggest long life, a dish which winds up every birthday feast, is placed on one side. A conical tower with steamed wheat flour biscuit occupies the other side. The shape of these biscuits is like that of the peach of immortality which grows in the western Paradise. There is also a pewter tray with mandarin oranges in the middle. The sound for the word orange is the same as that for lucky, and so the orange means good fortune. Around the mandarin oranges in separate compartments are the five seeds—the melon seeds, dried persimmons, dates, peanuts, and a fruit called dragon's eyes. These signify children, posterity. Below the table is a large urn for burning idol paper.

When all is ready the head of the household offers incense in the usual way while the members of the family stand about him. When he is through he burns the idol paper and the firecrackers are let off. There is no feast on this day. The offering is left for about half an hour and then is taken away.

At the temple of the Pearly Emperor there is a mass in which Taoist priests take part, or there may be theatricals.

And so for ages the Chinese have been reaching out after God, if haply they might feel after Him and find Him, though He is not far from each one of us : for in Him we live, and move, and have our being.

CHAPTER V

THE LANTERN FESTIVAL

The Lantern Festival occurs on the night of the first full moon of the New Year, that is the fifteenth day of the first month. It is called *shang yuan*, the first creative power. This power is the spring sun which warms up the earth and renews vegetation. The second creative power is the earth, whose festival is celebrated on the fifteenth of the seventh month. The third power presides over decay and is associated with water and the festival occurs on the fifteenth of the tenth month.

These three powers of nature, representing the renewal, growth, and decay of vegetation, and regarded at first as powerful creative influences or vapours, were personified in the course of time and worshipped as rulers over these seasons. A myth gradually developed celebrating their deeds. The Ruler of Heaven married the third daughter of the dragon king by whom he had three children, represented by the three creative powers. These rule the myriads of beings, and are assisted by 360 female gods. Thus we see that the three periods of the year as well as the days were personified and worshipped and various functions were assigned to them.

The festival being dedicated to the ruler of light is characterized by lanterns. These are made of a bamboo frame covered with paper and resemble vegetables, fruits, animals, fish, men, and numerous other objects. There are transparencies covered with silk gauze. Some have figures which are set revolving by the rising heat of the candle. Some are in the form of immense pumpkins. The dragon shape is quite prominent.

The streets are filled with holiday crowds. Poor indeed is the head of the family who does not purchase an assorted variety of lanterns for the children, and also as presents to the newly married brides. The present to the bride is made by her husband's parents and expresses the hope that she may soon be blessed with offspring. The term for lantern, *teng*, also means a man. In the city of Foochow the first year a lantern is presented with the motto "May Kuanyin (the goddess of Mercy) present you with a son". If the present has proved ineffective the following year a lantern with a picture of a child sitting in a wash bowl is sent. The third year a large lantern resembling a Mandarin orange with the words "May the child come quickly", is given. Usually other presents with similar suggestions are sent, such as sticks of sugar-cane, the name for which also means elder sister, a bowl of oysters, the name also signifying younger brother, or there may be two stalks of garlic whose sound suggests children.

The festival is celebrated by various contests. The sun returning from its southern journey meets opposition from the powers of darkness, and these contests were magic ways of assisting it. Nowadays, they help to break up the monotony of village life, though there is still a mysterious influence attached to them in many parts of China.

A favourite one is the contest between lions. Two men are covered with an imitation lion-skin, one of them being the head and the other the rear. Two such lions leap at each other and play all sorts of antics on a stage erected for the occasion. The lion is regarded as possessing great power to overcome

CONTEST WITH LIONS.

evil spirits which are especially active during this season of the year.

In the southern part of Fukien the festival is celebrated by an exhibition of roosters in the temple of the City Guardian. The rooster is the embodiment of the power of the sun because he announces his rising every morning and so a display of this harbinger of day is very appropriate at this time. The cocks are placed on tables in the temple with incense before them. The largest one occupies a place of honour and is popularly called " productive precious ". The neighbours congratulate the owner of the cock, considering this to be a good omen for success in business.

In Kuang Tsa in western Fukien the people place in a sedan chair an idol called the " fixed light suppressing tigers ". Over the chair they fasten light wires. With this they rush through the streets shouting, " Old Buddha." The wires give forth a humming noise. As the chair is hurried through the narrow, crowded streets the young fellows pummel each other on head and shoulders.

A favourite pastime is the manipulation of the dragon. A dragon 20 to 30 feet long is constructed in sections 3 or 4 feet in length, in which is a candle so suspended that it keeps its upright position regardless of the antics of the dragon. Each section is on a pole, and is carried by a boy. These boys are trained to manipulate the dragon gracefully sweeping through the streets and rounding corners. Before the dragon is carried a large globular lantern representing the spring sun which the dragon is trying to catch. Here, again, the drama of the returning sun is being enacted by the villagers with a view of bringing the sun back to the northern world safe and sound.

Another custom highly favoured in former times, but now fallen into desuetude, was that of erecting the "whale mountain". In a spacious public court a wooden structure resembling a mountain was built. Artificial grass, flowers, and trees covered the ranges. Tea houses illumined with lanterns were perched on its crags, or tucked away in its ravines. In the woods animals of all kinds roamed. The whole was illuminated with varicoloured lanterns and was a spectacle of surpassing beauty. Mountains are symbols of strength and longevity. The Book of Poetry says : "May your age be as the Nan mountain, which neither crumbles nor dies." The whale mountain symbolized at this time when the spring sun was returning with his power and freshness the prayer for strength and old age.

Stories of former days tell about the great ferris wheel, 200 feet high, erected in the capital of China in A.D. 713. The wheel was adorned with gold and silver flowers and lighted by 50,000 lamps. At a distance it resembled a flowering tree. The palace ladies, a thousand in number, were dressed in silk gauze, glistening with gems and kingfishers' feathers, and powdered with sweet powders. Maidens selected for their beauty adorned with flowers and with hairpins in their hair danced and sang below the wheel for three days and nights. The wheel represented the sun and symbolized his power.

The festival is also the opportunity to make appropriate offerings to the gods and ancestors who not only share in the joyful occasion, but are expected to do their part in fulfilling the prayers uttered at this season through the various symbols. The goddess of mercy, or the local mother goddess receive special attention, because they are the givers and protectors of children. These offerings are usually consumed by the members of the family after they have been spread before the gods who have partaken of the spiritual essence of the food, leaving the coarse material for the living.

The blessings asked are appropriate to the needs and occupations of the people. An old story from Honan tells about the experience of a man who saw at night a woman in the south-east corner of his house who addressed him as follows: "I am the spirit of the silk house of your family. On the fifteenth of the first month you must make an offering to me of broth and meat and as a reward I shall cause your silkworms and mulberry trees to increase a hundredfold." He followed her advice, and annually the people made an offering, and as they ate the food they repeated the words: "Ascend the heights with the broth, take away the rat plague, thou silkworm dame." The rats eat the silkworms and this goddess is supposed to protect them.

The day is also good for divining and prognosticating the future. Such matters as the weather, condition of the crops, the high prices of food, and other important matters may be foretold by the shadow of the moon. In Foochow the women place a skirt over the large lacquered night vessel. After burning incense and candles they utter their wish, and if it is granted the vessel moves.

In many households the family divines the future by popping rice. If the rice pops up making rice flowers it means good luck.

The official attitude toward these and other customs has been often hostile, though emperors and officials joined in the general celebration. No doubt the expenditure of money, the mixing of the sexes and the breaking of the decorum which is regarded as the ideal of the Confucian state as well as the occasion which such festivals gave for the committing of crime were deemed sufficient reasons to curb the people in their exuberant expression of joy. An official of the Sui dynasty (A.D. 589–618) memorialized the throne requesting the emperor to stop the riotous customs on the fifteenth of the first month. He said : " Every first month the fifteenth night crowds of people fill the streets and clog the cross roads, collect and play together. The sound of drums dins the ears of heaven. Blazing torches illuminate the earth. Men wear the faces of animals and don women's garments. Prostitutes and actors exhibit their tricks and strange shows. With ribald jests they make merry while men and women look on together. High platforms encroach upon the roads and bands of cloth over the streets resemble the clouds. The women are decked out in brilliant garments. Carts and horses clatter and crowd. Viands and wine abound everywhere. Stringed instruments and flutes make riot together. Wealth is squandered and property is wasted. The people vie with one another. The households pour out men, women, and children. The high and low, men and women mingle together. White and black are not separated. The result is immoral conduct, thefts, and robberies, and gradually the custom is fixed."

Alongside of this of the seventh century we may place the proclamation issued by the Manchu dynasty in 1910, a year before its demise : " The contests with dragon lanterns current in Fukien have in recent days given rise to much trouble and hence should be right speedily and sternly prohibited. And having received orders from my superiors I make this proclamation to soldiers and people that they may know that from the date of this proclamation they should burn all dragon lanterns in their possession. I do not permit them to amuse themselves with them nor to carry them in procession. If any dissolute fellows transgress this prohibition, I order forthwith to search them out and punish them. I decide to grant no mercy. All should fear and respect and not transgress. This is the purpose of the proclamation."

These proclamations have had little effect upon the celebrations. The spring calls and old custom calls aloud to the people to forget the dark, cold, dreary winter and to help the spring to come and bring its blessings.

CHAPTER VI

THE STORY HOUR

On the streets of Chinese villages on moonlight summer evenings the story-teller sets up his stand and recounts the old familiar stories to his audience which crowds about him filling the street. He tells about the early struggles of Mencius, or about Kuan Ti, the hero of the Three Kingdoms, or how the Goddess of Mercy visited Hades and by her presence was making it over into paradise when Yama, fearing the loss of his power, sent her back to earth. Quite often he tells the story of Lin Shui Nai, the mother goddess, who presides over the affairs of women.

Long ago in Chuan Chou, in south China, the bridge over the river was destroyed by floods and the numerous wayfarers had to be ferried over the dangerous stream. Often the rapid current swept away a boat-full of people and hurled them on the rocks below. The Goddess of Mercy, always solicitous for the welfare of men, was moved by this distress, and so asked the dragon king if anything hindered the rebuilding of the bridge. He replied that there was nothing to prevent this except lack of money. The goddess at once hit upon a plan to gather funds for this enterprise.

She transformed herself into a beautiful maiden, and a clump of bamboos she changed into a skiff. The local god of the ground she aroused from his dreamy existence in the village temple and made him her boatman. Then taking her place in the middle of the boat, she made the announcement that she was gathering money to rebuild the old bridge

and that he who could hit her with a coin could have her to
wife for a hundred years. The news spread like wildfire.
Young men, middle-aged men, old grey-haired patriarchs
came with their coins and tried to win this wonderful beauty.
The wealthy threw gold, some cast silver, and the poor tried
their luck with copper cash. Her magic power enabled her
to dodge every coin and at the same time to direct it that it
found a safe place in the boat. In this way a large sum of
money was collected for the bridge.

One day a seller of vegetables came along attracted by
the crowd. When he caught sight of the goddess he set his
baskets on the river bank, and took all his capital, pounded
the silver into fine powder, and filled his mouth with the
silver dust. Then he came as near as he could to the goddess
and spurted a silver shower over her. The silver dust spread
like a cloud about her. Some fell on her dress, some lodged
in her hair. The goddess, thus taken by surprise, took off
the headdress and threw it away, and transformed herself
into a cloud which slowly faded away.

The poor vendor stood upon the bank and saw the cloud
vanish into air and with it all his possessions and hopes.
In his despair he jumped into the river and was drowned.

The goddess and the poor seller of vegetables could not
thus escape their destiny. She entered the embryo of a
woman living in the suburbs of Foochow and was born in
due time. The soul of the vegetable seller was ordered by
Yama to be born in a poor but good family. He grew up
as an exemplary boy, received his first degree, being the ninth
on the list, and finally became a minor official. The goddess
and the man became engaged. The young woman, however,

had no heart for marriage. She delighted in burning incense to Kuanyin, and in reciting the sutras and gave herself to vigil and fasting. Her father became angry, smashed the image of the goddess, and tore up religious books. The young woman in her distress left home and went with an attendant to live in a monastery in the mountains of Lu.

On this journey she met her inveterate foes who were to test her life. One was a monkey in the guise of a man, and the other a snake. These two wanted to take her and her companion, but she threw her odorous beads at them and frightened them. They followed her to the monastery and found the words on the door, " Opened once in ten years." They knocked their heads against it. The words on the door were changed to " Opened once in a thousand years". They gave up their attempt for the time being.

In this monastery she lived the life of a common nun. She began with the menial duties of polishing rice. Then she studied the Buddhist classics. She was so diligent that her body was covered with characters which changed to eyes. After three years she completed her studies and decided to return home. Her teacher took leave of her and among other things warned her not to turn back in her journey. After walking twenty-four steps, however, prompted by her gratitude to her teacher she looked back. This disturbed him very much and so he warned her to be careful in her twenty-fourth year not to practise her arts.

At home she was joyfully received by her father, who repented of his previous sins and was now an ardent devotee. The match-maker began to complete the arrangements for the marriage with her fiancé. The two demons who dogged her footsteps were active again in their attempts to frustrate her purposes. Her future husband was now a candidate at the government examinations. One of the demons disguised as a servant filched his essay and dragged him to a cave in Kutien, where he drugged him with tea of forgetfulness. Then he tried to betroth him to a young woman in the cave. The young man remained loyal to his fiancé, but the demons then extracted some of his brains, and this left him helpless in their hands. The god of the soil, however, who is ever watchful over his domain, learned of the impending tragedy in the cave and quickly reported the distress of her lover to Lin Shui Nai. At first she suspected that this was another ruse of the demons to spirit her away and so she hesitated. Later the parents of the young man came to plead with her and so she planned her campaign. The father of her husband was instructed to fetch two loads of sulphur squibs and a jar of white wine mixed with sulphur. She also engaged several good spirits to assist her. The company amply protected by charms battered down the door of the cave, let off the squibs and squirted the mixture of wine and sulphur. The minor demons were killed, but the arch demon managed to make his escape. In the deep recesses of the cavern they found her betrothed hanging with his head downward. She resurrected him and brought him to her house. He soon recovered under her tender care, and the two were married amidst the rejoicing of all their friends and relatives.

The husband became an honoured official of the government and his charming wife was the guardian angel of the poor and distressed. But unlike stories in the West the real story begins after marriage. This goddess in disguise runs true to form. Among her many wonderful deeds the village fisher folk still extol her conquest of the sea monster. This immense fish appeared off the coast one day, and by its magic power created a beautiful palace with courts and balconies crowded with musicians and dancing girls. Its red tongue became a bridge and its two horns turned to masts. Its two eyes changed to lamps. Its teeth became monks. The people hearing enchanting music and seeing the beautiful palaces walked along the bridge into the monster's mouth and were devoured. Lin Shui Nai made a magic dagger, and by means of her occult arts, killed the monster and brought the people to life again.

At length she entered the twenty-fourth year of her life of which her Taoist teacher had warned her. The sadness of forebodings unknown crept over her. At first all seemed well, but one day the message came that her brother, a Taoist hermit, was ordered to pray for rain and being unsuccessful, was threatened with death by the hostile people. She was, moreover, soon to become a mother and was unable to help her brother while in this condition. The situation was critical and demanded heroic action. She resolved to help her brother, and so performed an abortion on herself and placed the embryo in a jar. In order to protect it from her old enemies she hung a sieve over the front door which was turned into the eight diagrams, a powerful charm. The bamboo dust pan she transformed into a gaping tiger. On the back door she tied a rope which turned into a snake at her magic touch. The house itself she changed into a lily pond. She put her mother in charge and strictly charged her to remain inside and answer no calls from the outside. She then departed to assist her brother in his efforts to bring rain.

The demons, the snake and the monkey, soon heard that Lin Shui Nai had left her embryo behind, and so they made plans to get possession of it and also to injure her. The monkey demon assumed the form of a little child and started out to hunt the house of Lin Shui Nai. He was unable to find the house and so returned and reported that instead of the dwelling he found a lily pond. The snake at once suspected a ruse and transformed himself into a bird and perched in a lotus flower and chirped. The mother, attracted by the continuous chirping, said, "If there is good news from my daughter let the bird call thrice." The bird called thrice and thus was assured that this was the house of his victim.

The snake at once assumed the form of a child and knocked at the door. The mother opened the door and seeing a child let him in. The child asked for tea and the mother sent him to the kitchen to fetch it. He went, but soon returned, frighted by the coiling snake. The mother unwittingly told him not to be afraid because that was only a rope. The child then wanted water and she sent him to the front door. He ran back frightened by the hungry tiger. The mother assured him that it was only a dust pan. Then he asked about the diagram on the door and was informed that it was only a sieve. Thus reassured the snake found the embryo and destroyed it and disappeared.

Meanwhile Lin Shui Nai had spread a mat in the middle of the river and was praying for rain. When her embryo was destroyed she felt a sudden pain in her abdomen and knew at once what had happened. Soon the snake and the monkey began to drag her into the water. She felt the rising waters and realized her danger and by a powerful charm called to her aid her teacher. He threw three stones into the river which became ducks and took Ling Shui Nai on their backs to shore. The strain on her was such, however, that she was broken in body and spirit and soon passed away out of this life.

After her death she became a goddess and aided those who were afflicted during childbirth and became the great protector of mothers and of all women in distress.

It is one of the interesting things about China that this goddess who mirrors the needs of women can be traced to a person who once lived and whose life and character are the basis of this tale. According to several records she was born in Foochow at A Do in A.D. 767. She married Lin Chi, and in her twenty-fourth year offered her embryo in order to bring rain during one of the most severe droughts which according to the records took place in A.D. 790, that is in her twenty-fourth year.

It took some time for the cult to obtain imperial recognition. Sometime between 926 and 935 she was granted the title, "The Lady obedient to Virtue" and also the "Merciful Helpful Lady". During the Sung dynasty between the years 1241 and 1253 the wife of the prefect after a pregnancy lasting seventeen months gave birth to several measures of snakes. The goddess was appealed to and brought healing. The prefect memorialized the throne and the goddess was granted the itle "The Great beneficent, illustrious, full of grace, merciful, helpful lady ". More recently the queen of Tao Kuang (1821–50) was advised during a difficult childbirth to make an offering to the mother goddess by a high official from Foochow. After a successful childbirth the goddess was given the title of " Ch'en the supreme Empress ".

The birthday of the goddess occurs on the fifteenth of the first month. At noon a bountiful offering is spread before her image in every home in Foochow. Among the articles offered are ducks' eggs, though a duck must never be offered because the ducks saved her from her enemies. The offering is made by the women and children who present the incense and bow and kneel at the alter in succession according to their age.

In the evening the temples of the goddess are crowded. Before her image is a vase of flowers. After burning incense the women take a flower and a stick of incense home. The flower stands for a child in metaphorical language and this not only suggests a child, but becomes a powerful force in bringing it. On this occasion the women give the caretaker of the temple thirty-three cash. The wealthy give a hundred and thirty-three. The sound of this number is similar to the phrase " give birth to ". Often the women take a shoe of the goddess with them. When the child comes this with a new pair of shoes is returned to the goddess as a thank-offering.

On the evening of the fifteenth processions in honour of the goddess are organized by the committee in charge of the temple. Characteristic of these processions are the floats with children representing the beneficent work of the goddess. The image of the goddess has a vase with flowers in her lap, which are taken by women as the goddess passes by.

The goddess occupies an important place in the life of women. Five months after a wife has conceived the husband returns thanks to the " mother goddess ". On this occasion an address is made as follows : " N. N. has begotten by his wife a child for these five months. He now presents these offerings as an expression of his gratitude, and begs that she may be protected during the rest of her time in good health and give birth to the child without complications. After this event takes place he will make another offering."

Near the time of delivery on a lucky day a special ceremony is performed to frighten away the monkey and snake demons who try to destroy the child. On this occasion the priest burns several crabs made of paper, or releases live crabs. The name of the crab resembles that of the demons.

In cases of difficult childbirth a puppet show is arranged in honour of the goddess. Three days after birth the child is washed and a thank-offering made to the goddess. Another is made when the child reaches the fourteenth day. At the age of one month the heads of girls are shaved before the image of the goddess, while the boys are shaved before the ancestral tablets. Offerings are also made at the age of four months and of one year. On this occasion the child is put in a large bamboo tray and before him are placed a pair of scales to weigh silver, a pair of shears, a foot measure, a brass mirror, a pencil with inkslab, books, an abacus, silver and gold ornaments and fruits. The object is to determine the future life of the child. Whatever he grasps at first indicates the trend of his life.

After this an offering is made to the mother at each birthday until the sixteenth, when the boy enters manhood.

Lin Shui Nai is not known by name outside of the province of Fukien, but she has her counterpart in every district and in almost every home. The needs and aspirations of women and the requirements of children have provided her altars with offerings and made her temples popular.

CHAPTER VII

THE TUTELARY GODS OF THE GROUND AND GRAIN

The oldest and at the same time the most popular gods in China are the gods of the ground and grain. Fashions in gods have come and gone, but these, after a history of several thousand years, have more temples and enjoy the worship of a larger number of people than any other deity.

The earliest records of the Chinese speak of the guardian god of the house. The early abodes of the people consisted of holes excavated in the loess river banks, or were constructed of grass and earth heaped upon a wooden frame. All of them had an opening in the roof for the smoke to escape. The ground under this vent, watered by the dews and rains of heaven and warmed by the sun, was sacred to the guardian deity of the place, called Chung Liu, "the place where the water drips in."

The early villages were built about an altar dedicated to the god of the soil. Under the Chou dynasty every twenty-five households were organized about a local altar and were called a *shê*. This character means the spirit of the ground, the social group about the altar. Nowadays it means society in the phrase shê-huei.

Throughout the history of China every political unit was under the protection of a local god of the soil. Under the last dynasty, the empire has a large altar in the southern city of Peking. Every provincial capital, prefectural city and district city had an altar dedicated to this god. The emperor had a personal altar in the palace grounds. These altars were square, varying in size according to the importance of the political unit. The emperor's altar was constructed with ground obtained from the different parts of his empire. Black earth represented the north, the red the south, blue the east, white the west and yellow the centre. Every village and usually every ward in the cities has its local temple; the graves have an altar to this god. Monasteries and temples have a shrine to the guardian of the place.

Following ancient custom the altars are surrounded by trees which were an evidence of the blessing of heaven and the survival of an ancient tree worship. The public altars are open to heaven and so represent the focal point of the fructifying forces of earth. The crude altar represented an early attempt of man to objectify the forces of the earth and relate them to his needs. It localized and fixed the spirit force of the earth. On this account the altars of a conquered dynasty were covered over so as to prevent the forces of heaven from revitalizing them and thus restoring the dynasty. These covered altars were used also for trials and places of punishment with a view to disrupting the magic gathered by the former dynasty.

About these altars was organized the life of the community. When the son of Heaven went on a journey he announced the fact to the god of the soil and made an offering for a successful outcome. Such matters as setting up of an heir apparent, sickness of the emperor, or empress, were announced at the altar. Here the soldiers starting on a distant expedition were exhorted to be true to the soil which gave them birth and nourished them.

With the god of the soil was associated the god of the grain. At first this was millet, that is, millet was the divinity to whom homage was paid. Later on a renowned ancestor was placed in charge of millet and worshipped at the same time as the god of the soil. The two are always spoken of together as the god of the ground and grain, She Chi.

The State offering took place on the *muo* day of the second month of spring and autumn, a day observed from ancient times to the end of the Manchu dynasty. Outside of the capital of the province shaded by ancient trees stood the simple square altar two feet high and twenty-five feet square with two terraces.

The high priest on the occasion was the viceroy, or the governor of the province assisted by all civil officials above deputy magistrates and all the military officers above a captain of a thousand. Three days before the offering they began to practise abstinence from highly seasoned foods, music, sexual intercourse and public business. The night before the offering the animals were duly approved and killed. The blood and the hair was buried in the earth.

The altar was then prepared. The tablets of the god of the ground and that of grain were placed on a table in the centre of the altar. Besides the usual incense, candles and flowers there were a goat, a pig, broth, two baskets with rice and millet, two vessels with panicled millet, four baskets with salt, dates, chestnuts, dried venison, four platters with turnip pickles, minced venison, celery, pickles, and minced rabbit. These were substituted by local products if they were not available. There were also goblets with wine made of millet and two rolls of white paper to represent silk. Near by was the official prayer on a table. At one side of the altar was a washbasin for the purpose of purification.

The position of each participant was fixed. The civil officials stood on the east side of the altar and the military officials were on the west side, the two groups facing each other. The ceremonial ushers, the reader of the prayer, the inspector representing the throne all had their places.

The offerings were first inspected by those who took part in the ceremony. This done the leader of the offering was led to the washbasin and washed his hands. The others took their places and the herald announced the offering which consisted in inviting and in receiving the gods to whom the offering is made.

The usher conducted the governor before the table with the tablets where he knelt. An usher on his left took the incense from the table and presented it to the governor who raised it three times to his forehead and gave it to the usher on his right. He was then conducted to his place beside the altar and all the participators performed the *k'ou-t'ou* (three kneelings and nine knockings).

The next offering called the first offering was conducted in the same way as that of receiving the gods only the offering consisted of the paper rolls and wine.

Following this the prayer was read by an official assigned to this task: " In a certain year, month, day, I, official, N.N., conduct the offering to the tutelary gods of the ground and grain. Only the gods pour out peace upon the nine grounds, provide grain to many lands, separate the five colours and so manifest the domains assigned to rulers. They nourish the husbandry of the hills, marshes and plains and promote sowing and reaping. Having received with reverence the charge of this locality I perform the sacrifice with respect. I trust that the land may flourish as luxuriantly as the pine and the cypress and that it may be established as firmly as the rock for all time, that the sprouting millet may ripen, that the gods will bless us with a full exhaustless granary in return for our worship. We hope that you will enjoy this offering."

After the prayer and a *k'ou-t'ou* the second offering was made followed by the third offering. Then the meal and wine of blessing were received from the gods as an earnest of the good things of the year. The gods were then sent away with due ceremony. The offerings were cleared off and the prayer and the paper rolls were buried. Then all retired.

The state worship has been in abeyance since 1912 and the altars have been neglected. The village god of the soil and his consort, however, are as popular as ever. Every village has a temple to the god. Some have just a little shrine with a bell and a tree. Others have elaborate buildings with dragons on the ridge. Besides the god of the soil and his retinue other gods have a place in the various niches: Kuanyin, the goddess of mercy, the goddess of small-pox, Kuan Ti, the god of war, and the god of the five roads.

The position of the god of the soil corresponds to that of a village constable representing Heaven above and the powers of Hades below. He is supposed to keep records of all that goes on in the village and report the same to Heaven and to the ruler of Hades. While customs vary, usually the announcement of births and deaths and other important events in the village is made at the temple.

The temple is governed by a committee appointed each year from the members of the gentry of the locality. This body has in its care the various festive ceremonies and also the financing of the same. The head of the committee is called "the Happy Head". The assessments are made according to the financial standing of the family and are usually paid in full. In case a deficit occurs the committee makes it up. Strict account is given of moneys spent upon a large sheet of paper posted on the temple.

The religious life of the village expresses itself in various processions, feasts, and offerings. In the first month the god and his consort are taken out on a tour of inspection through the village. At the end of a long line of men dressed in holiday attire, some beating gongs and drums, others playing flutes, carrying incense, holding boards with praises of the god, behind a flaming red umbrella, the sign of official dignity, comes the god seated in his sedan of state and borne by four bearers. People from other villages come in to see the sight and remain to the feast which follows. Such processions are said to bring peace and blessing.

In the villages about Foochow a custom is observed about the fifteenth of the first month called "keeping company with the gods during the night". Every family who has had something fortunate happen, such as the birth of a son or the promotion of a member to office, is assessed by the committee to make a special present called "joyous gold". This is used to provide the feast and theatricals. The temple is brilliantly lighted with lanterns and a bountiful repast is provided. After the offering made by the members of the committee, the people partake of a bountiful feast and enjoy the theatricals. The keeping company with the gods and eating with them is an old custom found all over the world. Such ceremonies connect the worshipper with his god and impart the strength of the god and keep away diseases and calamities.

Besides the regular offerings the god is invoked in difficult cases of childbirth. In times of pestilence, drought and other calamities masses are performed by Taoist, or Buddhist priests.

Connected with these religious ceremonies is the government of the village. The unit of Chinese life is the family and most of its affairs are settled internally. The common interests, however, centre in the temple. The temple committee make various regulations governing markets, the use of streets, street lamps, village policing and defence. They are for the village the law-makers, the judges and the administrative officers, of course always subject to the district magistrate.

The village is a self-governing entity. Villages often declare war on each other, capture hostages, make treaties of peace, and in other ways express their independent life. The village gentry often prohibit the export of grain for fear that the prices will be unduly increased. In this they frequently have the backing of the district magistrate.

The god of the soil still rules in the villages of China. His temples are found in the large cities also, for the large city is an agglomeration of village communities organized about the temple of the god of the soil. This organization is the most primitive and the most efficient. It has outlasted great dynasties and powerful rulers. It functions in modern Shanghai as efficiently as it does in far away Szechuan. It explains the duration of Chinese culture. These village communities each centred about the god of the soil are well governed and happy and they are the coral reef upon which the dynasties and rulers are built as islets. These come and go, but the villages function continuously and will ultimately bring quiet and peace out of the present chaos.

CHAPTER VIII
THE FILIAL PORRIDGE

One of the most popular festivals in Foochow occurs on the twenty-ninth of the first month. Every family prepares a gruel of glutinous rice mixed with sugar, peanuts, dates, beans, water-chestnuts, loquats, and almonds. This is offered to Heaven and Earth and the ancestors with appropriate ceremonies. It is also presented with other food to friends and relatives. On the surface of the gruel the character for longevity is worked out with peanuts, or other seeds. On this day the lanterns hanging in the house since the fifteenth of the month are burned with the hope that this will suggest to the spirits the desire for children. The word for lantern also means male.

The usual explanation given by the people is the story of Mu Lieng. His mother took the vow to eat no meat, but one day when she was very sick the son was told that a little meat would make her well and so he secretly introduced a morsel of meat into her food. On this account she was committed to the lowest purgatory after death. The son, stricken with deep sorrow, tried to bring food to her, but the demons guarding the door took it away from him. Accordingly he hit upon the plan of cooking up black objects with the rice. The devils deceived by the looks of the stuff let him pass. In memory of this filial love of Mu Lieng the people keep the present festival.

The festival is also called *hou chiu chieh* meaning the festival of the last nine, the others being ninth and the nineteenth.

After nine comes ten which means completion or the end. This day is regarded as dangerous to anyone whose age contains the number nine or its multiple. Accordingly such unfortunate people go to a friend's house and partake of his gruel. If they remain at home their friends send gruel. They must not eat that prepared by themselves.

Customs observed about the same time in other parts of China suggest still other explanations. In a district near Foochow the peasants call the gruel green broth and eat it for the purpose of bringing luck to their fields and of warding off disease.

In parts of Chihli province on this day the people make cakes and dumplings and hope to fill up the granary by this observance. They spread ashes mixed with grain upon the threshing floor and beat the grain bin. In other parts of the same province they beat the court about the house with a pestle and call it beating emptiness and want. On the twentieth day they make a picture of the grain bin on the court and place ashes mixed with grain upon it. The next morning they place the same into the granary. This act typifies replenishing the granary.

Similar customs are observed about this time in other provinces, and they seem to have a common purpose. This is to call the attention of Heaven and Earth to the fact that the grain bin needs to be filled again. The gruel offered to father and mother symbolizes the idea that this is no selfish prayer, but has in view the aged and the needy. The story of Mu Lieng is after all a good explanation. The peasant desires a good harvest that he may fulfill the primary duty of filial piety.

CHAPTER IX

THE GODDESS OF MERCY

The goddess of mercy, or Kuanyin, is the most popular deity in China. Her temples are found everywhere and her image has a niche in the women's apartments of almost every household. The name means "one who hears prayer". She hears the prayer of the needy, the oppressed, and those in danger, especially women and children. A very common title is "Great compassion and great mercy". Her other titles emphasize her power, her wisdom, but especially her great mercy toward all in distress.

She is represented in many forms. A common image is that of a beautiful woman with a child in her arms resembling the Virgin Mary. One of her titles further emphasizes this likeness by calling her the "ancestor of Buddha who hears prayer".

Kuanyin has had a long and varied history. Originally she was the Indian god Avalokitesvara, a male divinity, worshipped by the Mahayana School of India from the third to the seventh century of our era. This deity appeared as a Bodhisattva from ancient times in various places and under various forms, but always as a male. His favourite place was Potala, a mountain range east of Malaya. He was the protector of mariners and the saviour of the faithful from danger. He resembled Vishnu.

Avalokitesvara was brought to China by the missionaries of the Mahayana School, together with another Bodhisattva now worshipped at Wu T'ai Shan in Shansi and called Wenshu

GODDESS OF MERCY, KUANYIN.

or Mandjusri. In the transfer Avalokitesvara became Kuanyin and also became a female divinity. It appears that at first the god was a male. A work as late as A.D. 668 speaks of the god as a male only. In a collection published in the tenth century he is likened to a monk. In a collection of paintings published in the twelfth century, there are no pictures of Kuanyin with a woman's headgear, or garments. On the other hand, there is also evidence that in certain sections the god was a female very early. In the sixth century Kuanyin is referred to as a woman, and an empress in the same century who became a nun took the name Kuanyin. A song of the twelfth century praises her as follows: " Beautifully smiling and comely, beautiful shining eyes, the woman from the west."

When the change took place and why it took place is a matter still under discussion. Some hold that it is due to Christian influence, especially that of the Nestorian missionaries who established their work in China in A.D. 635. The whole subject is much broader than a question of contact of two religions. The virgin with a child is a conception which is pre-Christian; and so it is quite possible that the development would have taken place if the Nestorians had never come to China. But we are sure of this, namely, that the male and female form still survive and may sometimes be found in the same temple. A monk asked about this answered that a Bodhisattva was neither male nor female, and so could appear under whatever form seemed most appropriate. In this he had the authority of the sutras which claim the same power for this class of beings.

It is quite probable that in Kuanyin we have a composite

of the numerous local female deities which exist in all parts of China, together with the background of the Bodhisattva.

The books on Kuanyin are numerous. One popular to-day was first published in A.D. 1416, and republished several times since then. It gives the history of the goddess as an incarnation of Amitabha (Omi to fo) the god of the Western Paradise.

One day as Amitabha was sitting in the golden lotus enjoying his beautiful surroundings in the great hall of the Western Paradise, he looked afar with his kindly eyes upon all the beings of the eastern world. He saw the people blinded by their desire for wine, women, wealth, and fame, and steeped in their sins. Life seemed to them like a drunken stupor and death like a dream.

As he contemplated on the ways of the world, he realized that the men though sunken in their sins still had some knowledge of the three religions and knew what the good was, though they did not practise it to any extent. The women, however, did not even understand the course of heaven's doctrine, and the path of transmigration and the way of escape from the chain of existence. Amitabha, touched deeply by his sorrow, decided to be born in the world as a woman and show women what sin was and teach them how to repent and escape the sorrows of transmigration, the punishments of purgatory, and the guilt of the bloody pool (for those who die in childbirth) and lead them by example to ascend the road of enlightenment and to enter the Western Paradise.

Amitabha having made his decision to become incarnate as a woman, at once memorialized the Queen of the Western Paradise and received her permission to be born in the world.

He looked the world over, and decided to enter the royal family of King Miao Chuang, who ruled the country of Flourishing Forest located somewhere south-east of Asia.

One night the queen-mother saw the sun in her dream. Soon afterward she became pregnant and in ten months gave birth to a girl, whom they called Miao Chen. While she was carrying the child the queen abstained from meat. The little girl was very conspicuous for her goodness and beauty. Her intelligence was superior to others of her age. Once she read anything she never forgot it. From childhood she abstained from meat and milk, and gave herself to religious devotion and discipline.

At the age of sixteen her father decided to betroth her to the scion of a neighbouring kingdom, with which he desired to enter into closer alliance. Much to his surprise and mortification, she refused to obey and decided to give herself to a religious life. In his anger he compelled her to take off her court dress, to don the garments of a servant, to carry water, and to take care of the garden. She took up her menial duties with joy and with the help of the gods her work was made light and the flowers never looked more beautiful. The father repented of his anger and sent her two elder sisters to urge her to obey his wishes, but she remained firm.

The father then sent her to a monastery, and charged the abbess to treat her harshly, promising a reward in case she succeeded in converting the daughter to his plans. The abbess placed upon her the most menial tasks of sweeping the rooms, chopping wood, drawing water, and polishing the rice. She did her work well and did not become weary, for the gods assisted her. The abbess and the inmates urged her to leave this life of privation and hardship, but to no avail.

One day the rumour got abroad that the princess was associating with the young abbot of a neighbouring monastery, and that she had given birth to a child. The king, burning with shame and anger, attacked the monastery, razed it to the ground and put all the inmates to death. The daughter was brought before the king, and being still obdurate she was ordered to be executed; but the sword of the executioner was broken into a thousand pieces. Finally she was strangled, but immediately a golden image appeared on the spot and her soul joined the spirits of light.

The Queen of the Western Paradise learned of the fate of her protégée and immediately sent a holy man who ordered tigers to take her body to a pine forest. Her soul was brought to the Western Paradise.

She was then permitted to visit purgatory, but her benign presence began to change this place of woe to a paradise. Yama fearing that he would lose his kingdom at once hurried her to the upper world.

In the meatime her body was guarded by the gods in the pine forest. When she returned from her pilgrimage to purgatory she resumed her body and entered the monastery near her father's capital. The father, now an old decrepit man, was sick and his body was bursting with virulent ulcers, one for each of the five hundred monks he had put to death. Heaven had ordered also that his life was to be shortened by twenty-four years for his sins. He came to the monastery and the old monk told him that he would become well if he could obtain an eye and an arm of a blood relative and mix

THE LAUGHING BUDDHA.

them with medicine. The king offered his realm to his two daughters for these members. They were ready to sacrifice themselves, but their husbands would not permit them. The monks then advised a life of abstinence and as a penance urged the restoration of the monastery and provision for services to ferry the five hundred monks through the other world. One day at the monastery the king found hanging on an altar an eye and an arm. These were boiled and mixed with medicine and rubbed on the ulcers. The father became well. Later he learned that these members belonged to his young daughter whom he had strangled. This deepened his penitence. He turned over his kingdom to his officials and gave himself to a religious life. His daughter became Kuanyin. Thus Amitabha completed his incarnation by showing his filial piety to a father who rejected the daughter. She is really the incarnation of the greatest virtue of the Chinese, filial piety. Kuanyin now may be found in the temples with Amitabha, the Buddha of the Western Paradise, and Ta Shih Chih. The three are called the three holy ones of the West and are well known as saving people by bringing them to the Western Paradise.

Kuanyin is not merely a goddess who is worshipped for her mercy to women and people in distress. She reveals future events to her devotees and issues frequent exhortations to the people of China in the form of little booklets which are given away without cost.

The Goddess of Mercy is worshipped by the faithful on the first and the fifteenth of every month. She is worshipped by special ceremonies on the nineteenth of the second month, her birthday, on the nineteenth of the sixth month when she became a Bodhisattva and on the nineteenth of the ninth month when she put on the necklace, or as some say when she died. On these days offerings of vegetables are made to her. A month after marriage the young bride receives from her parents an image of the Goddess of Mercy with a censer and a pair of candlesticks. A special offering is made at any time of need as in droughts, floods, and pestilence.

Kuanyin is the ideal of Chinese womanhood. Her images are admired by men and worshipped by women. She is beauty, gentleness, and mercy personified. She watches over all who are in danger. She is the patroness of women in all their concerns and is especially invoked in cases of childlessness and danger at birth. She occupies the central place in the hearts and lives of the women of China.

CHAPTER X

THE GOD OF LITERATURE

The Chinese have always regarded writing and literature as the gifts of Heaven and have held in high honour those who embodied ideas in beautiful literary form. It is no wonder then that Wen Ch'ang the "God of Literature" or the "Emperor of Glorious Literature" occupied a high place in the Chinese pantheon.

The story of this god will illustrate the way gods come into existence and attain power and then are cast down from their high place to make room for others. The Chou dynasty (1000–255 B.C.) worshipped a god of the centre who was located in the stars of Ursa Major. This deity ruled over blessing, revenue, and old age and was worshipped by burning a pyre under the open sky. The Han dynasty (206 B.C.–A.D. 221) worshipped the same group of stars. Later times selected six stars from the Ursa Major and associated with them various functions of the government. One, called the great general, ruled over the army, the second called the prime minister ruled over the affairs of this official. The third controlled ceremonies and literature. The fourth was over the revenue. The fifth called ruler of destiny was in charge of portents. The sixth had supervision of robbers, and was the patron of the tribunal of justice. The offering to Wen Ch'ang took place on the first day after the winter solstice with the cyclical character *hai*. This day was observed until the Manchu dynasty, which set the sacrifice on the third day of the second month and a lucky day of the eighth month.

Under the Sung dynasty the emperor Chen Tsung (998–1022) gave Wen Ch'ang the title "The tutelary god of destiny of the nine heavens, the exalted one of Heaven who protects life". His consort was given the title of "The great holy queen of the azure heaven". The god of destiny and his consort, the tutelary god of the centre and the god of revenue were given places on the altar of Heaven. Still later he was given the title of Ti or emperor.

During this time, we do not know just when, the god took on human form and was born in Tzu T'ung. The stars in Ursa Major became his heavenly palace, and on earth elaborate temples were erected for him. Under the last dynasty there was an official temple in each capital of the province, prefecture, district, and chou. Besides these, numerous temples were supported by the gentry. The city of Foochow had about forty such temples.

The temples and images were kept up in good style. The image of the deity, modelled on a prosperous scholar and official, was dressed in a blue garment embroidered with dragons. On his right was an attendant called "Earth Dumb", and on the left "Heaven Deaf". The latter was in the garb of a Taoist doctor, and had his hair done up in two knobs. He held in his hands a record of the graduates at the examinations and the felicitous gem which endows the owner with power to attain whatever he wishes. The phœnix is the messenger of this satellite and he rides upon a white horse, i.e. fleecy clouds. The titles of these companions were suggested by a passage in the Analects in which Confucius shows that Heaven accomplishes its work without any ostentation. They were a warning to scholars not to pride

OLD EXAMINATION HALLS AT NANKING
(These have been torn down and the material used in building modern schools).

themselves on their accomplishments, but to imitate the powerful silence of Heaven and Earth. Before Wen Ch'ang was usually the image of K'uei Hsin, another god connected with literature. Both of these images had a high place in the homes of the old literati.

The temples of Wen Ch'ang were the club houses of the literary men of the neighbourhood. Here they met to discuss their affairs and to hold their poetical contests. Here offerings were made on the birthday of the god, the third day of the second month, followed by joyous feasts in which the gods participated.

The god, even to-day, occupies a high place in the hortatory literature of which the Chinese are so fond. He is the medium through whom Heaven reveals its will upon the moral and religious questions of the day. This may be done by means of the planchette, or by the more mysterious way of dropping a volume containing the message from Heaven.

The present generation of students are worshipping other gods and preparing to build other temples. The temples of Wen Ch'ang have been turned into schools, or serve as centres for social gatherings. The images are crumbling and the god who once occupied a palace near the God of Heaven in Ursa Major is disappearing from the memories of men.

CHAPTER XI
K'UEI HSIN

The Chinese have a proverb: "Men without gods get along right well, gods without men tumble down pell mell." Such has been the fate of this patron of literature and of the old literati. Still he has behind him a long history and the present may be the chrysalis stage of a future still more glorious.

K'uei Hsin is the name of the stars *alpha, beta, gamma*, and *sigma* of the Great Dipper which the Chinese call the northern peck. These stars form the head of the peck and so the term K'uei means head or chief. In ancient times the north pole was even nearer to the Great Dipper than it is now and to the Chinese this constellation seemed to direct the stars and the seasons. In the spring it pointed to the east, in the summer to the south, in the autumn to the west, and in the winter to the north. The character which designates this group of stars is composed of the character for peck (tou) and the character for spirit (kuei), and so the whole means the tutelary spirit of the peck.

At first this constellation, or the tutelary spirit of it was worshipped, not as the patron of literature, but as the regulator of the stars, of seasons, and of human affairs. Sze-ma Ch'ien calls *alpha* the hinge of heaven about which all things revolve, *beta* was called the armillary sphere, *gamma* the planetarium, and *sigma* the balance of Heaven. A little later these stars were regarded as ruling the *yin* and *yang* principles of nature, calamities, and punishments. The first star was especially associated with the emperor. Thus gradually the literary class, which was also the ruling class, found its ideals embodied in the tutelary deity of this group of stars, and the cult of the K'uei Hsin became well established.

Under the last dynasty this god was pictured as a being with two horns and a terrible red visage standing on a sea-monster with one foot and the other raised in the air. The sea-monster is probably the azure dragon, the constellation Scorpio, which the handle of the Dipper seems to touch. The god held a pencil and the seven stars of the Dipper in his right hand and a cap of honour and an ingot of silver in his left. These were the insignia of office. He used to preside at the state examinations.

The god was canonized in A.D. 1314 by the emperor Jen Tsung of the Yuan dynasty. It is related that the god took on human form and appeared at the highest examinations of the Hanlins. When the emperor saw his ugly face he refused to give him the golden flower to which he was entitled. The god, in his disappointment, jumped into the water, but the tortoise came to his assistance and he mounted the sky and became a god of literature.

Under the Manchu dynasty the name of this god was used to designate the successful candidates who took a high rank in the examinations for the second and third degrees. A special offering was made to him on the third day of the second month at the time of the spring offering to the God of Literature. In literary households incense was burned before his image or the characters representing his name on a piece of red paper on the first and fifteenth of each month, and also whenever a general offering was made to household gods.

The old examination halls have disappeared. Modern school buildings are rising in their place. The crowds of students who used to flock to the examination cells and burn incense to K'uei Hsin and Wen Ch'ang are no more. A new company with different ideals and with a different spirit has taken their place. Still the god survives in many a house and ancestral temple. He will probably go the way of Pan, but he will not die, but undergo a transformation and adapt himself to modern conditions.

CHAPTER XII

LÜ TUNG PIN

Lü Tung Pin, another patron god of literature, differs from Wen Ch'ang and K'uei Hsin, in that he is a historical character. He is one of the Eight Genii who occupy a prominent place in Chinese art and mythology. He belonged to the numerous anchorites who lived in the mountains, by the streams and lakes, and in the deep recesses of the forests, and who regarded the mythical emperor Huangti (2697–2597 B.C.) and Lao Tzu as their patriarchs.

The purpose of these hermits was to attain to long life and immortality. They lived a life of self-denial, eating as little food as possible, and breathing in as much air as they could. The food is produced by earth and belongs to the principle *yin* and to death. Hence the less one eats the farther away he gets from death. The immortal had no need of food at all. On the other hand, the air belongs to *yang*, the male principle of nature. The more that one can inhale and the more he can retain without exhaling the more of life and immortality he has. Some of these old worthies breathed through the pores of their skin and one is reported to breathe through the heels.

Not only did they try to free themselves from such earthly things as food, but all selfish desires, all self-seeking, fleshly lusts, lust for power and fame and wealth were suppressed. The attempt was made to imitate the Tao which had no private selfish purposes of its own, but was actuated by unselfish love in all its actions. These men had given up high office, they had left their wealth, they abandoned home and the comforts of civilized life and retreated into the wilderness to live the simple life.

To the absence of all possession they added the highly regarded quality of inaction. They were quietists and cultivated the quiet life. The Tao did not strive to accomplish its work and yet because of this activity in inactivity all things were done well. The emperor Shun ruled the empire by sitting on his throne facing the south and he ruled it well. So likewise these hermits sought the activity within inactivity.

At first these anchorites had high ideals, but they lost them in the course of time and tried to achieve immortality by discovering the elixir of life, by various breathing exercises and bodily contortions. They all practised the occult art of medicine and were the pioneers of this profession. They collected herbs and so helped to establish the science of botany. They also were more or less expert in various arts of disappearing and appearing in out of the way places.

Their great ideal was to get to the Western Paradise presided over by the Queen of the West, which was located in the high ranges of the Kun lun. On the east the Pun Lai islands, probably Japan, were also considered the Isles of the Immortals.

Among this class of beings, occupying a middle ground between the gods and men, patriarch Lü belongs. He is usually spoken of as one of the eight of the immortals or genii, six being men and two of them women. Some Chinese scholars place the origin of this classification into the Yuan dynasty.

He is known as Lü Yen. His public name is Tung Pin.

He was born in the year A.D. 755, on the fourteenth day of the fourth month in Honanfu. If we may believe his personal history, he was no common babe. When he was born a white crane came to the house. A strange odour filled the room. His body resembled metal, his head was like that of a crane, his back like that of a tortoise, his body resembled the tiger, his cheeks were like those of a dragon, his eyebrows like those of a kingfisher. In fact, he resembled many animals who are noted for special powers in the mythology of the Chinese.

In due time he grew up, received the first, second, and third degrees, and then became a magistrate in the district of Teh-hwa in the province of Kiangsi. He used to go into the Lu Shan, a mountain range south of Chinkiang. Here he met Chung Li K'uan, who is the first and greatest of the eight immortals, and is said to have lived during the Chou dynasty.

Lü offered himself to spread the true doctrine among men. Chung Li K'uan was not sure that he was equal to this great task, and so tested him by ten temptations.

1. Lü returned home from a long journey and found his family all dead. Lü's heart was not grieved, nor distressed, but made preparations for burial. The dead came to life again.

2. Lü was selling goods. The price was already agreed upon when the purchaser went back on his bargain and offered one-half the agreed price. He left both the goods and the money in the would-be purchaser's hands and took his departure.

3. Lü went out on the street on New Year's Day. A beggar asked him for alms. He gave the beggar money, but the latter was not satisfied, and so reviled Lü and presented him with

a knife, a very unlucky omen. Lü took the knife and thanked the beggar, who jeered at him. Lü then took his departure undismayed.

4. Lü was keeping sheep in the mountains. A tiger came to steal the sheep. Lü put the sheep into a safe place and then drove the tiger off.

5. At one time he was reading in a mountain hut. A beautiful girl came by. She said that she had lost her way and was weary, and wanted to stay. For three nights she tempted him, but he came off victorious.

6. One day, while away from home, his property was all stolen and he had nothing to eat. He was not angry, but took a hoe and dug for his living. Suddenly he saw under his hoe ten pieces of gold. He covered them up and did not take one of them.

7. One day he bought a quantity of brass-ware. When he came home he found it was all gold. He returned it all to the merchant who sold it.

8. A Taoist priest was selling medicine which was guaranteed to kill in ten days the person who took it. Lü swallowed it and remained hale and strong.

9. The river had overflowed its banks. Everywhere people were wading through the water. Lü was in a small boat. The wind was high and the current was strong. He sat upright in the boat without fear of death.

10. One day while he was sitting alone in the house hundreds of goblins and devils jeered at him. Some wanted to beat him and some wanted to kill him. He asked no questions. Again a large number of evil spirits came with a dead criminal. The soul of the man was weeping and saying that Lü had

killed him and now Lü's own life was demanded. Suddenly there was a voice in the air. The devils vanished and he saw the patriarch Chung Li K'uan.

Having thus passed these tests Lü was given a sword and was sent out to do 3,800 good deeds in the world. He went up and down killing tigers, dragons, and ridding the world of various evils.

In the twelfth century temples were erected in his honour under the title of Ch'un Yang (Mayers' *Chinese Reader's Manual*, p. 158).

He is usually represented with a sword by which he destroys covetousness and anger, love and lust, trouble and anxiety.

He is also the patron saint of the barbers. It is difficult to say just what his standing with the new barbers will be. Their implements and methods are taken from the west and it may be that this new class may forget the patriarch Lü.

CHAPTER XIII

THE FEAST OF COLD FOOD

This feast is called *han shih*, meaning eating cold food, because the Chinese in days gone by extinguished the fire in the kitchen for a few days and ate cold food. It is also called *ching yen*, "forbidden fire." It comes before our Easter, and two days before the Ch'ing Ming festival. It is not observed at present and so belongs to the fossilized festivals.

The custom of extinguishing fires at this time of the year was observed in ancient China. According to the Chou Li, "The officers in charge of fire, in the second month of spring, made their rounds sounding a wooden rattle in order to enforce the extinguishing of fires." The wooden rattle survives to this day and is sold on the streets for a few cash. The vender goes along the street sounding it in order to attract the children of the neighbourhood. We find similar rattles sold just about Easter time in different parts of Europe. These playthings, found in localities separated by such long distances, refer to customs similar in purpose.

This custom of putting out fires in the spring is found among worshippers of the sun. The time of the vernal equinox, according to the view of primitive man, is a critical time for the sun. The powers of darkness and death are especially active, and the spring sun struggles against them valiantly. There are not wanting at this time, however, signs of his victory. The willows are sending forth their buds and the grass is putting forth its green blades. The knolls and hillsides turned toward the sun are green with the fresh verdure of spring. The powers of darkness and death make a last attempt to extinguish the sun by the equinoctial storm, but after the storm the sun smiles more brightly than before and the pure clear wind comes.

Primitive man feels that he, too, has a share in this struggle between the sun and the powers of darkness. Not only is his happiness dependent upon the victory of the sun over the powers of death, but he believes that by his actions and his ceremonies he is able to help the sun in this great struggle. From this arise a large number of customs observed in different parts of the world, but possessing in common one and the same functional purpose, namely, assisting the spring sun in his struggle against darkness and death.

The best way of assisting the struggle was to extinguish the fire in the stove and eat cold food for several days. This was done from very ancient times. According to the Chou Li the custom was enforced by the government. By the time of the Wei dynasty (A.D. 471–532) the tenacious observance of the custom caused such mortality among the young and the aged that it was forbidden by imperial edict in A.D. 474. The law could not be enforced, however. The custom was forbidden in the district of Chieh, Shansi, and permitted elsewhere. Soon after the custom was forbidden there was a violent hailstorm in which many people were killed and the crops were damaged. This calamity was attributed by the superstitious populace to the imperial decree which forbade them to extinguish their fires and so the custom was reinstated in A.D. 496.

During the T'ang dynasty, A.D. 618–907, and during the Sung dynasty, A.D. 960–1278, the emperors distributed at the time of this feast burning sticks of elm and willow to the officials near the throne. This was done to harmonize the *yang* vapours. It is also reported that the children of servants in the imperial kitchen vied with one another in producing fire by friction. The one who obtained fire first ran to the emperor and was presented with rolls of silk and a metal bowl.

The popular tradition attaches the custom of extinguishing the fire to Chieh Chih T'ui. According to the Tso Chuan, Wen Kung, the prince of Tsin (B.C. 696–628), the present Shansi, had a faithful follower called Chieh Chih T'ui, who shared the prince's exile in 654 B.C. When the prince returned to power in 635 B.C., Chih T'ui declined all reward and in order to escape the prince's urgency he disappeared in the forests of Mien Shan. The prince searched for him, but could not find him and so changed the name of the mountain to Chieh Shan. Thus far the Tso Chuan.[1]

According to a later legend, the prince set the forest on fire in order to drive him from his hiding place; Chih T'ui clasped hands with his mother about a tree, and perished in the flames. During the third month, when this happened, fires were forbidden and food was eaten cold. This is the story related to-day in explanation of the feast. We have seen, however, that the explanation is quite different.

Numerous other customs practised at this season in different dynasties and in various places will serve to illustrate the origin and the significance of this festival. Among these is the custom of colouring eggs. Kuan Tzu, who died B.C. 645, writes: " Colour eggs, boil them, and break them. This

---

[1] This mountain is in Shansi, on the boundaries of three districts.

is whereby we bring out that which has been accumulated and stored up. This is an emblem of dispersing and distributing all living things." Just as the life is stored up in the egg, so it is in the earth and at this time the victorious sun breaks the shell and brings it out from its dark abode.

In Foochow, at present, dumplings are made with peppermint chopped up and mixed with rice or other vegetables inside and symbolize the same idea as the eggs.

The kicking of the shuttlecock, which is now a favourite pastime of school boys in China, probably originated here, though the invention is also attributed to the emperor Huangti (2697–2597 B.C.).

The swing and the merry-go-round found in certain parts of China have their origin here. The motion originally was intended to assist in the struggle of the spring sun. The history of the province of Shantung describes the festivities of Shou Kuang Hsien. "Two days before the Ch'ing Ming they forbid fires and tread upon the green grass. They make a place for theatricals. Some act their plays in theatres. Others dress up as female magicians and beat drums. Men and women gather like clouds. The roads are clogged with noisy people. The householder places two timbers into the ground in the garden and hangs up a rope with a board on it, making a swing. This is what people of the T'ang dynasty called the amusement which brings the sensations of being an immortal. Also in the market places they plant a large piece of timber several tens of feet high. At the end of this they fasten a wheel. To the spokes they fasten curved boards suspended by ropes. Below a large piece of timber is placed transversely. Men push this around. Women gaudily dressed whirl around through the air. Red and purple fly about shimmering like hundreds and thousands of butterflies. The dust flies. This is done by the lower and the middle classes. These things show a lack of instruction in the family."

From early times the people observed the custom of going to the suburbs of the cities and treading upon the green grass. In Foochow during the Sung dynasty a garden located near the yamen of the prefect was opened and the people enjoyed the flowers. Those who went out brought back herbs and roots which, picked at this time, had special medicinal value. In the country districts to-day they bring back pine branches and stick them beside the door. These represent long life.

A few days before the festival the people stick willow branches under the tiles at the edge of the roof. The willow, which comes out very early, symbolizes the power of the spring sun in revivifying all nature and overcoming the powers of death, and hence its universal use on this occasion in China. In Europe and America, the pussy willows are brought to the Catholic churches on Palm Sunday and blessed by the priest.

From ancient times the elm and the willow were used to kindle the new fire after the day of the cold food. This was called changing the new fire. He who did it received blessing for the whole year. In certain parts of Chihli the saying is: "He who does not wear the willow, though a young man, will become a grizzly head." A passage in the history of Chihli says: "At this season (i.e. Han Shih) the people are sad at the beginning of spring. Every year they await the time when the elm and the willow send out their leaves and they pick them and regard them as grain."

Another custom observed in Peking throws light on our interpretation. On the Ch'ing Ming day they begin to sell ice. They take two small bronze cups and beat the ice. Here we have symbolized the destruction of death.

In these ways the ancient Chinese tried to assist the annual re-birth of nature and so expressed the longing for the mastery of death and of the life beyond, which the yearly progress of nature symbolizes. To-day only the name Han Shih survives to give us the clue to the intimate connection which these men used to feel they had with nature.

CHAPTER XIV
THE CH'ING MING

The Chinese divide the year into twenty-four seasons *chieh ch'i*, which means the nodes or breathings of nature. The season of Ch'ing Ming, "Pure and Clear," comes after the vernal equinox, one hundred and six days after the winter solstice, and follows the festival of cold food, beginning about 5th April and ending 20th April. The struggle between the *yang*, the power of light, and *yin*, the power of darkness, has ended in the victory of light. According to the Book of Rites the Chinese have tried to assist this process by offerings. " The son of Heaven sacrificed a male goat. He broke the ice and offered it at the ancestral temple." The male goat reinforced the *yang* and the breaking of the ice symbolized the defeat of the *yin*. The air at this time is pure and the light is clear.

The victory is shared not only by the living, but also by the dead who rest upon the hillsides. Every one instinctively turns to his departed ones. The old and young go to the graves, pull up the dried grass and weeds, paint the letters on the tomb-stone and then spread an offering on the ground to the dead and to the guardian spirit of the tomb. A little of the wine is poured on the tombstone. When the dead have partaken the living sitting near the tomb consume the food.

If the family has been visited by sickness and misfortune this is often attributed to the unhappiness of the dead. On the advice of a geomancer they take out the coffin and re-bury

it in a site better favoured by the wind and water influences.
In case the coffin has rotted they take out the bones, scrape
them off, and wrap up in silk batting and bury on a new site.
Those whose relatives have been buried during the past year
weep at the grave.

The people not only go out to care for the dead, but also
to receive into themselves the energy of spring by treading
on the green grass and feeling the rejuvenating power of the
vernal air and sunshine. They pluck branches of the pine,
the emblem of long life, and place them at the door of their
house.

Willow branches are also inserted under the tiles of the
roof above the door of the house. The people relate that
during the T'ang dynasty a general was about to rebel against
the emperor and so instructed those loyal to him to put
willow branches over their doors. This happened on the day
of this festival and so has been kept up as a custom. The
willow is one of the trees endowed with power of *yang* and is
placed above the door because it is supposed to oppose evil
influences which are not entirely subdued.

In recent years the Christian church has recognized the
values of this festival, and is conserving them by filling them
full with the message of eternal life as revealed in the
resurrection of its Founder.

CHAPTER XV

PLOUGHING THE FIELD

Agriculture has been the chief occupation of the Chinese for many thousand years. In the enumeration of the different classes into which Chinese society is divided the farmer occupies the second place. It is not surprising, therefore, that agriculture found recognition on the part of the emperor and his officials in all parts of China by the ceremony called ploughing the field. This ceremony took place in the second, or third month of spring.

The custom of ploughing the field has the sanction of the Li Chi where we read : " This is the month in which the son of Heaven on a favourable day prays for a good harvest to Shang Ti. On a lucky day the son of Heaven takes a plough and places it between the military officer in charge of the shield and the driver of the chariot. He conducts the three superior ministers of State, the nine secondary ministers, the princes and the grand prefects ; he takes the goblet and says : ' Drink the wine as a reward of your labours.' " This ceremony has been followed by succeeding dynasties. It was usually preceded by a sacrifice to Shen-nung, the divine husbandman who invented the plough, discovered the medicinal value of plants, and established markets for the exchange of produce.

The sacrifice to Shen-nung took place outside the east gate. According to the regulations his altar was two feet one inch high and twenty-five feet wide. The god was represented by a tablet two feet four inches high and six

PLOUGHING IN SOUTH CHINA.

inches wide. The base on which the tablet stood was five inches high and nine inches and a half wide. The tablet was red, and on it were the characters in gold, " The spirit of Shen-nung." Behind the altar was a small temple in which the tablet, agricultural implements, and sacrificial vessels were kept. Before the altar was a public field four and nine-tenths mow, or about three-fourths of an acre, in extent.

The ceremony took place in the second, or third month of spring on a day which was denoted by the cyclical character *hai*. It was performed by all the civil and military officials above the deputy district magistrate and the commander of a thousand men. In Foochow the viceroy, or the provincial treasurer officiated. Two days before the event the officials practised abstinence. The altar was swept and repaired. On the day of the sacrifice the proper officers placed a table in the centre of the altar facing south. Upon the table they arranged thirteen dishes with broth, grain, and fruits. Before the table were two large trenchers, one with a goat and one with a pig. In front of these was a small table with an incense burner and candles and the prayer to the god. To the east of this table was placed a table with one roll of paper to represent silk, a vessel for libations, three winecups, the sacrificial meat, and the sacrificial wine. There was also a basin with water. The officials took their places before the altar. The viceroy, or his deputy went to the altar and raised the incense given to him three times while kneeling. The ceremonial usher read the prayer, which was as follows: " Thou, Spirit, didst originate planting and reaping. Thou didst establish all the people. We extol thy inventive power. Thou art associated with Heaven. We remember thy merit, which nourishes all beings. We exalt thy name in mighty song. At this time the activities of farming begin. All men gather in their ancestral fields. Great art thou, for ever the exalted emperor performs the ceremony of ploughing three furrows once a year. Reverently he guards the soil. He does not presume to forget the toiling husbandman, and so offers sacrifice respectfully and performs the ceremonies. We hope that there will be wind every five days and rain every ten days. May we continually receive thy Spirit's benevolent gifts. Then we shall have nine heads on one stalk of wheat and each head will be a double one. May our good fortune cause us to record continually a bountiful harvest. May our sacrifice be enjoyed."

When the sacrifice was over, the officials changed their official dress and went to the field. The ox was harnessed to a plough. The viceroy took hold of the plough with his right hand and the whip in his left. A farmer dressed in a palm fibre raincoat led the ox. The viceroy proceeded a step or two and turned the plough over to a farmer who made nine furrows across the field. Then the viceroy took the hoe and dug up the ground nine times. This done, the officials arranged themselves before the altar. The ceremonial usher gave the order to kneel and bow. They performed the k'ou-t'ou. The ceremony ended, the calvacade returned home.

By this simple ceremony the emperor and his representatives all over the empire held the plough with their magic touch and thus made agriculture for the year possible for the peasant.

CHAPTER XVI

THE GREAT YEAR

The Great Year, T'ai Sui, is no other than the genius presiding over the star Jupiter. Like other people the Chinese believe that the stars control the phenomena on earth. Rise and fall of dynasties, the birth of great men and of little ones, calamities and good fortune are determined by the stars. The histories of China usually began with a map of the heavens indicating the stars which presided over the different provinces.

Among the stars Jupiter early assumed an important place and that not because of its size, or its distance, for the Chinese knew little about that, but because of the fact that its sidereal period is about twelve years. In fact it is only 11·86 years, but this slight difference did not trouble the ancient Chinese. The Great Year is then the year of Jupiter and this star was regarded as the ruler of time. The year, the months, the twelve constellations of the zodiac, the twelve hours of the day were ruled by this key star.

The Chinese early invented the twelve branches or duodenary cycle of symbols and combined these with ten stems. Each of the branches and stems is represented by a character and the combination has given sixty pairs of characters or the cycle. In early times these characters of the cycle were employed to designate the days. Beginning with the year 103 B.C. the Chinese applied the cyclical characters to denote the years. The branches have corresponding animals and the stems correspond to the different elements, wood, fire, earth, metal, and water. At present each unit of time, year, month, and day hour is denoted by two characters of the cycle.

Jupiter represents father time who creates and destroys. His agents are the years, the months, the days, and the hours. These agents control and work through the five elements and the twelve animals and the constellations with which these are connected. The different elements produce each other as water produces wood, or they destroy each other as fire consumes wood. The animals likewise are friendly, or hostile to one another. Granting then that Jupiter stands at the head of this system, and that every event is controlled by the year, month, day, and hour in which it happens we have here the basis of an elaborate system of astrology.

In the temples this system is represented by images. One of the courts of the temple of the city guardian at Foochow is devoted to Jupiter and his retinue. Jupiter, an image dressed in yellow garments, with a black beard, a necklace of skulls about his neck and a fan in his hand occupies the place of honour in a glass enclosed niche. The skull necklace is a symbol of his authority over the life of man. A little to his left behind the niche are three small images about a foot high representing the present year, last year, and next year. On each side of Jupiter are six images, representing the twelve months or branches. Next to these are pictures representing the twenty-four seasons. In books, though not in this temple, the days and hours also are represented by presiding genii. Thus the whole system is dramatized so that even the illiterate may understand it.

AN OFFERING TO JUPITER, THE RULER OF TIME.

Jupiter then is the head of this complex system in which man is but a cog, but a self-conscious cog who understands the machinery and may use it to his advantage. In fact by means of various magic means he may overcome an evil situation by arraying against it the opposing elements of the system.

From early times calamities such as famines were attributed to the influence of Jupiter. This god had to be placated if the household was moved, or if a building was erected, or the ground disturbed. His special sphere, however, was over human life and destiny. Through the spirits of the days he metes out rewards and punishment. If a man is sick the doctor may decide that his trouble is due to disregard of Jupiter and so he advises an offering on his next birthday. In Foochow a man, or a tiger cut out of paper is placed on the table as a substitute into whom the disease will be sent. There are also cock's blood, a raw egg, and a piece of raw meat. After the service the substitute is burned, and the egg and raw meat are intended for the tiger who takes the disease away.

The new astronomy is dethroning Jupiter, but it will take some time before it can dethrone the sense of mysterious destiny which has used Jupiter as a symbol.

CHAPTER XVII
THE SHEPHERD'S PURSE

On the day before the third day of the third month the people of Foochow fasten small bouquets of shepherd's purse tied with a red band to each side of the outer door of the house. In case there has been a death in the family the band is blue. This is called in the local dialect the Ci-ci-chai, this being the name of the weed. It is also called He-ci-chai, meaning "the shepherd's purse put up by Her Majesty's orders".

The popular story is that once there was a rebellion somewhere in this part of the country. The imperial troops were coming to punish the rebels. It so happened that the family of one of the royal concubines lived in this same region. She was anxious to save her people and so she agreed upon the shepherd's purse as the sign which would enable the general of the army to distinguish between her family and the rebels. The relatives of the concubine told their friends and neighbours about the sign and they in turn told others. When the general arrived he found shepherd's purse on every door. He returned without punishing anyone. To remember this happy occasion the people place shepherd's purse upon their doors on the third day of the third month when this event happened.

In the books the festival is known as *shang szu*. The character *szu* is the sixth of the twelve branches. These branches from early times were combined with the ten stems and used to designate the days of the month. Each month there were three days which were denoted by the character *szu* and the first of these days was called the upper or first *szu*. The Chinese divide the year into twelve seasons also and denote each of these by a character which characterizes the season for which it stands. The season which runs over into the fourth month is called *szu*. According to the Shuo Wen A.D. 100, "*Szu* means that in the fourth month the *yang* or male vapours have already come forth and the *yin* vapours have been hidden away." Sze-ma Ch'ien says in his Shih Chi, "*Szu* means that the *yang* vapours have attained their completion." The character *shang* placed before the *szu* means the first, the upper *szu*. By the third day of the third month the *yang* vapours have not attained their full completion, but the victory over the powers of darkness and death is assured. The *yang* vapours have pervaded all beings and are driving out the *yin* vapours which represent death. The significance of this festival is then that the sun which represents the powers of light and life is victorious over the powers of darkness and death.

The festival is very old. The Chou Li says : "The female *wu* (sorceress) had charge at proper seasons of the year of driving away evil spirits by means of washing in perfumed water." The great commentator of the Han dynasty, Ch'ing K'ang-ching (A.D. 127–200), explains this passage to refer to the same custom as that observed in his time on the first *szu* day of the third month. It was also observed in the autumn. The Chinese did not wash their bodies during the winter. When the weather becomes warm the clogged pores produced disease. The ancient Chinese explained this in a different way. The male principle entered the body and drove out the female principle which represents disease. This excretion on the body had to be washed off.

During the Chou dynasty and during succeeding dynasties the spring ablutions to wash off the *yin* excretions were quite common.

There is a passage in the Analects about the bathing in the spring. It also throws light upon the ancient ablutions accompanying the ceremony of capping which took place when the adolescent passed over into full manhood and received the cap worn by full-grown men. Confucius asked his pupils to state their ambitions. One after another stated his great ideals. At last Confucius turned to Tien and asked him to state his ambition. Tien said: "I like at the end of spring, when the spring garments are adapted to the weather in company with five or six young men and six or seven lads to take a swim in the I river, then cool off in Wu-yün mountain and then sing awhile and return home." The master sighed and said, "I am with you, Tien."

During the Han dynasty there was observed on this day a custom of feasting in the water. This was common in Foochow during the Sung dynasty (A.D. 960–1278). The feasters formed themselves into a circle in the water and as the cups floated toward them they partook of the wine. This was called calling back the spirits of the dead. This is another allusion to the victory of light over darkness, and of life over death.

To-day the people still say that by fastening the shepherd's purse they drive away evil and bad luck. Some boil it and wash the children who have been affected with skin diseases in it. The community action no doubt imparts confidence and the ablutions are a preparation for other sanitary measures suggested by modern hygiene.

CHAPTER XVIII
EMPIRE AND RELIGION
MA TSU P'O, THE GODDESS OF THE SEA

From very early times the Chinese thought of the earth as a square surrounded by four seas each presided over by a tutelary spirit. According to the "Shan Hai Ching Yü", written as early as the Chou dynasty (1000–255 B.C.) the god presiding over the northern sea was called Yü Chi'ang. His face was like that of a man and his body like that of a bird. Suspended from his ears were two green snakes; twined about his feet were two green snakes. The guardian deity of the eastern sea, Yü Hsü, had yellow snakes suspended from his ears and twined around his feet. He was said to be the son of Huangti (2697–2597 B.C.) and the father of Yü Ch'iang, the guardian deity of the northern sea. On an island in the southern sea there was the spirit Pu T'ing Hu Yü having the face and body of a man with two green snakes in his ears and two red snakes around his feet. A similar spirit guarded the western sea.

The worship of the seas has a long history. Yao and Shun (2356–2205 B.C.), the Confucian ideals, made offerings to the four seas. According to the Li Chi the son of Heaven authorized proper officers to offer sacrifices to them. From the Han dynasty on (206 B.C.–A.D. 220) we find frequent mention in the dynastic histories of these offerings. By the time of the T'ang dynasty (A.D. 618–907), the worship was firmly established. The guardian god of the eastern sea was worshipped at Laichow in Shantung, that of the southern sea was worshipped at Canton, that of the western sea in T'ungchow in Shensi, and that of the northern sea in Honan. Commerce was expanding and the seas were growing in importance. During the T'ang dynasty the southern provinces were incorporated into the Chinese empire and the great task of assimilating and civilizing them was begun. In this process religion had no small part. Accordingly in the year A.D. 781 the gods of the four seas were given the title of King. The importance of the southern sea, that part of the ocean south of the Yangtze, to the northern Sung dynasty (A.D. 960–1127) is reflected in the new titles granted to its tutelary deity. To the title of King was added that of Holy in the year A.D. 1040. When the leader of the pirates infesting this sea, Nung Ti-kao, ran away in the year A.D. 1053, this was regarded as due to the efforts and assistance of the King of the southern sea, and he was granted the title of "The Great, Holy, Universally Assisting, Refulgent Gracious King".

Up to the end of the Northern Sung dynasty (1127) the guardian gods of the four seas were regarded as males but in 1123 the tutelary god of the southern sea was regarded as being a female.

This change in the sex of the god is due to several forces which converged to produce the goddess of the sea, Ma Tsu P'o. She was born on a small island called Meichou, in the district of Hinghwa on the coast of the province of Fukien. Her father was the scion of an official family tracing its ancestry back to the T'ang dynasty. Both father and mother were pious, did good works, dispensed alms, and worshipped the goddess of mercy. When the father was over forty years old he was sad because he had no son to succeed him and so day and night he and his wife burned incense and prayed Heaven for a son. One night Kuanyin appeared to the wife in a dream and gave her a pill, saying that Heaven had heard her prayers. The wife swallowed the pill and in due time gave birth to a daughter to the great disappointment of her husband. This was in the year A.D. 960, the third month, the twenty-third day. Other dates for her birth are given by various authorities.

When the girl was born a ray of rosy light entered the house from the north-west and a strange odour filled the room. For a whole month the babe did not utter a cry and so she was called silent. She surpassed other girls. By the time she was eight years old she could read and explain the classics. When she was ten she enjoyed burning incense and repeating Buddhist sutras. When she was thirteen she was instructed in the occult arts by a famous Taoist doctor. When she was sixteen she went according to the local custom to gaze into the well and was presented by a spirit with a brass charm.

She was able to sit on a mat and cross the sea. She mounted the clouds and roamed about the islands. The villagers called her the dragon maiden. She was able to transform herself, drive away evil, and save men from danger. She did not marry. In the year A.D. 987 on the ninth day of the ninth month, she was translated, and began her career as a goddess.

Some say that she jumped into the sea in order to save her father and brother in great danger. Whether this is true or not, it is quite probable that she must have done something out of the ordinary in order to impress the people of her village and the surrounding country. At any rate after her death the villagers built a temple dedicated to her and worshipped her. Her cult spread among the seafaring population on the coasts of Chekiang, Fukien, and Canton. This is not an isolated phenomenon. In Foochow the " mother goddess " was born in the year A.D. 767, and her cult is quite popular in Foochow at the present day.

For many years the cult of the goddess of the sea was a local cult quite separate from the worship of the four seas instituted by the different dynasties. When the rulers of China began to turn their attention seriously to the southern part of China they adopted the local goddess of the sea and gave her a place in the pantheon of the State religion. From that time her cult developed side by side with the expansion of the Chinese empire southward. We are able to see in the titles bestowed upon her the importance of the southern provinces and the outlying islands to the Chinese Empire. From this point of view these titles are not merely grandiloquent phrases, but are the embodiment of the strivings and ambitions of the rulers for an empire which shall include not only the mainland, but also the islands of the sea. In other words the development of the goddess of the sea is connected with the economic and political struggle for an empire.

In the year A.D. 1125 the Kin Tartars established a kingdom in north China at first locating their capital at Liaoyang and later at Peking. They turned their armies against the Sung dynasty, compelled it to vacate K'aifeng, its capital, and by the year A.D. 1127 they practically controlled the country north of the Yangtze river. The Sung dynasty made Nanking its capital, and from now on is called the Southern Sung ruling the country south of the Yangtze. Kao Tsung, the first emperor of the Southern Sung, instead of fighting the Kin Tartars himself, called in the Mongols, whose ancestral home was around Lake Baikal. The Kin Tartars and the Mongols fought together, the latter coming out victorious under the leadership of Kublai Khan, who turned his armies flushed with victory over the Kins against the tottering Southern Sung dynasty and conquered it, making his capital at Peking in A.D. 1280.

When the Southern Sung dynasty was confined to the country south of the Yangtze river it came into closer contact with the southern provinces. It recognized that the cult of the goddess of the sea was an important factor in the local life of the people. The dynasty also realized that the goddess of the sea was an important factor in the larger national life in the conquest of the outlying islands, in the subduing of the pirates and the overcoming of disease and pestilence. In the course of time various events were associated with her.

In the year A.D. 1123 Su Yun-ti on his journey as ambassador to Corea was overtaken by a great storm. Seven out of the eight vessels of his fleet were lost. His ship was saved near the island of Meichow. The captain and crew attributed their salvation to the goddess of the sea who appeared to them during the storm dressed in red garments. Lu memorialized the throne and the goddess was given the title of " Favourably assisting to cross the sea ".

Not only did she save shipwrecked ambassadors, but in the year 1159 a great typhoon which destroyed many pirates who infested the landlocked bays on the coast of Fukien was attributed to her. She also saved the people from a severe pestilence and so she was given the title of " The lady who is powerful and merciful and clearly answers prayer ". In A.D. 1192 she assisted the people in a great drought and received the title which means a royal concubine. During the Southern Sung dynasty A.D. 1127-1280 in ten of fourteen titles granted her she was called the royal concubine. These titles were bestowed as recognitions for services against pirates, help in shipwreck, drought, and pestilence.

Kublai Khan had dreams of a great empire embracing China and the islands on its coasts. He established his capital at Peking which was then, as it is now, unable to support its great population. He needed food from the south to feed his armies and retainers and so reconstructed the Grand Canal and extended it to Tientsin. The tribute rice could pass safely up to Peking by this inland waterway without being intercepted by the Japanese pirates on the coast. He organized an expedition to Japan which ended in failure. He sent his armies to Cambodia and Burma. Here he achieved better success, but the tropics proved his deadliest enemies just as they did to the hordes of Jenghis Khan who poured into India. In all these expeditions, he depended upon the southern provinces for ships, supplies, men, and a safe base for operations.

We are not at all surprised to find that the cult of Ma Tsu keeps pace with the progress of the empire southwards. In the year A.D. 1278 two years before Kublai became emperor of China, he gave Ma Tzu the title of " Concubine of Heaven ". This was an advance on the Sung dynasty. Within the short time which the Mongol dynasty of Kublai reigned over China

(A.D. 1280–1341) the goddess of the sea was given titles at five different times, always for some meritorious service to the nation. Temples were built for her by the Government and official sacrifices were made to her. The Mongol dynasty favoured Buddhism, and it is quite probable that this made them well disposed to this goddess who resembled Kwanyin.

During the Ming dynasty (A.D. 1368–1644) the southern sea became more important to China than before. Tonking was annexed as a province during the reign of Yung Loh (A.D. 1403–25). The Portugese reached Canton in A.D. 1516 followed by other European nations. They were always ready to turn their hand to piracy when legitimate trade was dull. From A.D. 1522 on the Japanese pirates made frequent visits to the coasts of China and pillaged the wealthy cities. Outside the Water Gate of Foochow are numerous tumuli which contain the bodies slain in one of these encounters with the Japanese pirates.

Hung Wu, the first emperor of the Ming dynasty, added the title "holy" to the previous titles bestowed on the goddess. He ordered that her worship should take place in the second month of spring and autumn. The emperor Yung Loh built a temple for the goddess which was called a palace. He ordered incense to be burned to her on the first and fifteenth of each month and a special sacrifice on the twenty-third day of the third month, the birthday of the goddess. These sacrifices were performed by the Board of Public Worship.

The Manchu dynasty raised the goddess of the sea to the highest position, calling her T'ien Hou, the queen of Heaven. A sacrifice was made to her in the second month of spring and autumn. Incense was burned on the first and the fifteenth of each month by a deputy of the local official. At the sacrifice a prayer was read which gives us an insight into the position of the goddess. The prayer is as follows:—

"In the year of —— day —— I, N.N., holding the office of —— make a sacrifice to the exalted spirit, the Queen of Heaven entitled 'Assisting the dynasty and protecting the people, Answering prayer with wonderful power, With boundless love assisting every place, Blessing and aiding all beings, Exercising a powerful influence on all the sincere'. Only thou, Shen, Buddha, transformest thy body, thou art holy and powerful, thou art the lord of the four streams, thou dost hold the seas within their shores, thou dost still the waves, quiet the winds, thou dost enable the boats to carry their cargoes safely. Relying upon thy merciful love, in obedience to the imperial will, I respectfully make an offering. We have all come here in the second month of spring (or autumn), respectfully presenting the odours of the platters. We ardently desire the goddess' protection and aid, so that the seas may be calm and the rivers pure."

The temples of Ma Tsu P'o, the Queen of Heaven, are found everywhere in the coast cities of Chekiang, Fukien, and Canton. They are well built and well kept up by a local committee of merchants. The goddess is usually placed in a large niche and is surrounded by painted clouds and carved dragons. On her head is a crown with jewels and pendants. She has on a rich red garment embroidered with golden dragons. In the hands she holds a jade tablet which used to be carried by the ministers, for the purpose of taking notes. In the hands of the goddess it signifies that she is able to come to the very throne of high Heaven and present her requests there.

The goddess of the sea has two satellites. One, at the right of the temple as one enters it, is dressed in red. He holds his hand before his gleaming and staring eyes looking off toward the horizon. He is called "the eye of a thousand li". On the other side of the entrance is a figure in blue, who has his hand placed to his ear. He is called the "ear of the favourable wind". Both of these are symbolic figures indicating that the goddess has means at her disposal to see danger and bring relief speedily. The colour of their garments is that of the lights on the foreign ships. In the back of the temple is a large platform on which theatricals are performed on her birthday, the third month, the twenty-third day, and also on the ninth day of the ninth month, the day when she was translated.

The Chinese merchants who move to a city from other districts usually establish a guildhall which is the centre of their common life. In these guildhalls, located in the coast cities, Ma Tsu P'o occupies a prominent place.

The modern steamers which ply between the ports of China, the launches on the inland waterways, the junks and sampans almost all have a little niche for the goddess of the sea. On a voyage, morning and evening, incense is burned to her. On her birthday, and the day of her translation, there is a special offering with a feast. The introduction of steam into China waterways has not in any way diminished the prestige of the goddess.

When a person is about to start on a long journey over the seas, he makes inquiry of the goddess by means of the bamboo divining blocks whether his journey will be successful. The traveller takes a pinch of the ashes from the incense burner before the goddess and sews them up in a small bag which he wears on his person as a charm against evil. The women desiring children consult the goddess.

In the year 1912, the first year of the Chinese Republic, the official offering was omitted, and the popular celebration was not as imposing as formerly. The goddess has passed through many vicissitudes. She displaced the Lords of the four seas who in their turn displaced the early mythological beings of foreign origin mentioned in the " Shan Hai Ching ". It will be interesting to see what influence the modern age will have on this ancient cult.

CHAPTER XIX
T'AI SHAN

T'ai Shan, the most famous of the sacred hills of China, rises 5,060 feet above the Shantung plain north of T'aian. At present each of the three religions of China has temples and monasteries on its peaks. In the spring of the year thousands of pilgrims throng thither for the purpose of worship.

The cult of the mountain T'ai Shan is connected with that of the five sacred mountains representing the five directions. T'ai Shan represents the east, Hua Shan in Shensi represents the west. According to the popular belief it rules over metals, birds, four-footed beasts, and reptiles. Heng Shan in Hunan represents the south. Another mountain, also called Heng Shan, in Chihli represents the north. During the Chou dynasty (1000–255 B.C.) Sung Shan in Honan was added to represent the centre.

The Chinese historians all agree in assigning the offerings to T'ai Shan to the dawn of Chinese civilization. The Supplement to the Shih Chi, written during the first century B.C., says that T'ai Hao who ruled China 2852–2737 B.C., and whose capital was in Ch'en (now in eastern Honan), made an altar on T'ai Shan and offered a sacrifice upon it to the tutelary spirit of the mountain. Kuan Tzu, fifth century B.C., and the Book of Records contain numerous notices regarding the sacrifices to T'ai Shan by the early emperors of China. The founder of each dynasty made an offering to T'ai Shan. Many emperors offered special sacrifices to the mountain when they changed the title of their reigns.

T'ai Shan was worshipped by the Emperors because it was regarded as the guardian of the empire. From very early times, moreover, the mountains were looked upon as the abode of the clouds which produce the rains and the streams which water the plains and which enable man to cultivate the soil and live in peace and plenty. T'ai Shan has attained its predominating position among the five sacred mountains because it is situated in the east. The east belongs to spring which is considered to be the source of life. The Azure Emperor of the east and the Azure Dragon, which consists of the constellations of Virgo, the Balances, and the Scorpion, also rule T'ai Shan. The star Jupiter also is looked upon as being over T'ai Shan. From its position as the source of life, it was not a long step to the idea that T'ai Shan rules men's lives, determines the station which men occupy in life, fixes the length of life, happiness, and misfortune and rules over the spirits when they have left this life.

We shall first consider the State sacrifices to T'ai Shan and then the popular worship of the god. The sacrifice took place in the spring because T'ai Shan is viewed as ruler of life, which has its origin in the spring. At first the sacrifice was made on a square altar under the open sky. Often the sacrifice was made at some place distant from the mountain, but facing its direction. As yet there were no temples. In the T'ang dynasty (A.D. 618–905) we find temples to the tutelary gods of the mountains and streams. In these T'ai Shan was worshipped. At the beginning of the Ming dynasty (A.D. 1368–1628) a large temple to T'ai Shan was built at Nanking. At the present time the temples to T'ai Shan are very numerous and some of them are built on a magnificent scale.

COURT OF T'AI SHAN IN HADES.

During the T'ang dynasty (A.D. 618–905) and perhaps earlier, images were made of T'ai Shan. We read that T'ai Tsu of the Sung dynasty (A.D. 960–76) prayed to the mountains and streams for rain. After the rain came, as a thank-offering he ordered clothing, a crown, a sword, and shoes to be made for T'ai Shan. During the Ts'in dynasty in the state worship in the sacrifice to Earth T'ai Shan as well as the other sacred mountains were represented by tablets. In the temples of T'ai Shan, located in all parts of China, there are magnificent images of T'ai Shan, his queen and concubines, his eunuchs and his adopted sons.

The objects offered have varied from dynasty to dynasty. Ming Ti (A.D. 227–40) offered a bull, a goat, and a pig. In the time of the northern Wei dynasty (A.D. 386–532) jade and silk were offered. The Ming dynasty offered a bull, a goat, and a pig and five kinds of fruit. The Ts'in dynasty followed the Ming dynasty. Musical instruments were employed at the sacrifice and a prayer was offered. The following is the prayer used in Foochow during the Ts'in dynasty. "In the year —— the month —— the day —— official N.N. makes a sacrifice to the exalted spirit of T'ai Shan, the Eastern Mountain. The Holy Dynasty rules the empire and remembers kindly the hundred gods. Thy spirit's power bestows blessing upon the whole province of Fukien. Thy place is in the Eastern mountain. The exalted power of the mountain descends to earth equalling heaven. It sends the clouds and the rain. All beings flourish, the seasons are fruitful. It blesses kindly all peoples. Enjoy the thank-offering which we dutifully and reverently offer in the second month of spring (or autumn). Receive the sacrifice. The myriad of blessings come from thy power. Descend, come nigh, and receive our humble offering."

T'ai Shan, like other gods of the State pantheon, has been granted titles in recognition of his meritorious services to the State. In the reign of Yuan Tsung (A.D. 725) the title of "The King who harmonizes heaven" was conferred on him. As this emperor was on his way to the mountain a strong wind sprang up and tore the canopy of his chariot and snapped the poles supporting it. The attendants said that this was done by the spirit of the eastern ocean who came to receive the emperor. When the emperor came to the altar a cloud surrounded it and while the instruments played, a favourable wind wafted in from the south. When he sacrificed to the chief tutelary deity of the mountain, a five-coloured cloud appeared and the sun was encircled by a halo.

In the reign of Chen Tsung (A.D. 998–1023) the mountain was given the title of "the Loving Holy King who harmonizes heaven". Later the same emperor gave the god the title of "the Loving Holy Emperor who harmonizes heaven". The god's consort, of whom we hear for the first time, was given the title "Illustrious Virtue" and the god was presented with proper ceremony with the document containing these titles. In the Ming dynasty the title was simplified to "The Spirit of the Eastern Mountain T'ai Shan". These titles are found in the temples of T'ai Shan at the present time. In its ritual the Ts'in dynasty used the title "The Exalted Spirit of the Eastern Mountain T'ai Shan".

Besides the regular worship there were sacrifices offered when an important event was announced to T'ai Shan. The birth of a son, the determining of the heir to the throne and the change of the title of the reign were announced with due ceremony to the tutelary deity of T'ai Shan. Whenever the emperor passed by the mountain he stopped to make an offering.

The State worship of T'ai Shan cannot be separated from the popular worship which must have begun very early. We have already noted that T'ai Shan ruled over men determining the length of their life and good and bad fortune. He also ruled over the spirits of those who died. These two functions made his cult very popular among the people. When Buddhism brought its ready made Hades, this function of T'ai Shan was made much clearer. The Po Wu Chi which contains matter dating to the third century A.D. says that T'ai Shan " is the grandson of the Ti of Heaven (i.e. the emperor of Heaven). He rules the summoning of men's souls. He knows the length of man's life ". In the books of the Later Han dynasty (covering the period A.D. 25–220) we find this statement made by Hu Chung. "I was very sick for three years and did not become better. Then I went to T'ai Shan and inquired regarding his will in respect to my life." Luh Ki (A.D. 261–303), a commentator, poet, and military commander wrote a poem on T'ai Shan in which occur these words : " On a distant peak he summons ten thousand spirits. In his chamber of the gods he gathers a hundred souls."

From these quotations we see that T'ai Shan was not only the ruler of man's destiny while on earth, but that he ruled the fortunes of men after death. This function was more and more developed until at the present day we find him in charge of the seventh court of Hades. This position in Hades makes him powerful in the world of men. Hades is an old institution in China. The social life is so organized that it needs Hades. We find mention in the Southern History which deals with events from A.D. 420 to 529 of eighteen hells. This would show that Hades was well developed at that time and hence its origin must belong to a much earlier time.

It will help us to understand the position of the god and the scenes depicted in his temples if we describe the court of hell over which he presides. The substance of the description is taken from a work entitled Yü Leih Ch'aou Chuen Ching She, a popular treatise on the ten courts of Hades. The introduction in my copy is dated A.D. 1809. The book is very popular at present and may be purchased for a few cents. The seventh court of hell is at the bottom of the great ocean north-west of Wo Chiao Shih. It is called the hot vexatious big hell. It has sixteen small hells. (1) Where the body is beaten until blood comes and then the person is compelled to drink it. (2) The hole where the thighs are burned by fire. (3) Where the breast is divided. (4) Where the hair is pulled by a prong with teeth. (5) Where dogs eat the shin bones. (6) Where the person sits with his legs crossed while a stone presses the top of his head. (7) Where the crown of the head is beaten and the head cut open. (8) Where there is distressing and painful barking by dogs. (9) The place where the skin is cut and pulled by pigs. (10) Where the wild pig and wild goose gnaw and peck. (11) Where the feet are bound and the body hung up. (12) Where the tongue is taken out and the chops are pierced. (13) Where the intestines are taken out. (14) Where the donkey tramples and the male wolf or wild bear eats the flesh. (15) Where the fingers are branded. (16) Where the body is put into a caldron of boiling oil.

The following persons are consigned to this hell. Those who concoct medicine of woman's monthly flow, or of the placenta ; those who drink wine to excess ; those who steal children and sell them ; those who take clothing and ornaments from coffins ; those who take bones from coffins for the purpose of making medicine ; those who separate close relatives ; those who sell girls taken into the family as future brides of the sons to become prostitutes ; those who permit their wives to drown baby girls ; those who expose children born out of wedlock to die ; those who form a clique and gamble and divide the profits and cause the losers to hang themselves ; the teachers who harm their pupils by being too lenient with them ; those who beat without cause male and female slaves and thus cause them serious injury ; those who treat neighbours as though they were fish and pork, i.e. use them for their own selfish purposes ; those who disobey their elders ; those who cause strife by taking secretly both sides of the controversy.

This then is the hell over which T'ai Shan rules and such are the people who are punished therein. We notice that those who do violence to the human body go to this hell. T'ai Shan rules over life and in hell he presides over that department where sins against the body, especially those which cause the body to die, or employ dead bodies for medicine, are punished.

The temple of T'ai Shan situated outside the east gate of Foochow is famous throughout the province. It was especially popular among the Manchus. The most wealthy and prominent literary and official families both among the Manchus and Chinese had representatives on the committee which managed the temple. T'ai Shan was a magnificent gilded idol with a crown of jewels and a yellow robe. He had wives and concubines, eunuchs, a crown prince and several adopted sons, ministers, messengers, and runners. In the dark corners were realistic representations of parts of the court of Hades over which he presides. Everything was on a most magnificent scale.

The high class Manchu and Chinese women formed a society for the purpose of dressing the queen and the chief concubines. Several days before the great procession in the spring they met in the temple premises and washed the faces of the female idols, arranged their hair, and dressed them. They usually spent several nights each year at the temple. These societies, for there were several, had diplomas which were given to those who had served as apprentices. They were very exclusive and only the members of high families were eligible for membership.

At one time over forty different societies were connected with this temple. These societies were formed for the purpose of planning the procession of T'ai Shan, or the crown-prince, or one of the adopted sons or some idol in the temple. They collected funds which they invested in fields, or houses, and from the proceeds they financed the processions and the feast which followed.

These processions, arranged on a regal scale, took place on the twenty-fourth day of the third month in the southern suburb of Foochow and on the twenty-fifth day in Foochow City. Along the line of march each household set up tables with incense and offerings. T'ai Shan was preceded by the retinues of the crown prince and the adopted sons, by the big devil so called and the small devil; there were eunuchs, lictors, long lines of well-dressed men carrying incense followed by men with baskets of flowers and offerings. At last in a sedan chair of imperial yellow borne on the backs of sixteen men in yellow garments came the great T'ai Shan. As he passed there was a deathly silence and everybody's countenance was reverently directed toward him. That night he was lodged in a large wealthy house especially prepared for him at great expense to the householder. The next day the magnificent procession wound its way through Foochow City. When the idol was brought back to his temple there were theatricals and feasts for several days for the participants in the ceremony.

It is said that beautiful young women did not come out to see the procession because they were afraid that the idol might take a fancy to them and compel them to become his concubines. A story is related of a butcher whose beautiful daughter became sick and in her delirium said that T'ai Shan had called her to become his concubine. When she died the father filled with grief and frenzy ran to the temple of T'ai Shan and slashed the idol's head. The Chinese say that the cut could never be fixed.

The temple of T'ai Shan was visited yearly by thousands who made vows in behalf of a sick father or mother, grandfather, or grandmother. The filial son prepared himself by abstinence and went to the temple with a chain around his neck, or a cangue, or handcuffs on his hands, dressed in red garments worn by criminals, and carrying burning incense and kneeling every few steps on the way. When he arrived at the temple he stated his purpose before the idol and inquired whether his wish would be granted. Before he returned he was given a charm on a yellow piece of paper to ward off evil influences. When the wish was fulfilled and his father or mother became well he made another trip to the temple to thank T'ai Shan.

The idea that sickness of the parents is due to the sin of the children is quite general in China. The son by carrying the cangue, or chain about his neck and wearing red garments takes the punishment upon himself and lifts it from his loved one who is being afflicted.

The temple of T'ai Shan at Foochow has passed through very trying days during the revolution. Soon after the battle of Foochow the students organized a regiment several hundred strong for the purpose of going north to fight the Imperialists. This regiment was quartered in the temple of T'ai Shan. The boys occupied their leisure hours by practising decapitation on the idols. T'ai Shan's head was severed and his jewelled crown disappeared. The wealthy committeemen were requested to contribute toward the expenses of the regiment. After the departure of the regiment the head-men of the surrounding villages organized a school in the temple.

The disturbed conditions have interfered with the annual procession. But T'ai Shan is still the lord of the seventh hell and as long as the sanctions of the other world are needed he will occupy his unique position.

CHAPTER XX

THE INAUGURATION OF SUMMER

One of the twenty-four seasons of the Chinese year, called the beginning of summer, begins about 5th May and is regarded as a time when special precaution should be taken to adapt oneself to the changing vapours of the season and in this way to assist nature to pass this period without difficulty. The characteristic feature is the struggle between the *yang* with the *yin*. All of the customs are supposed to harmonize both principles so that evil influences will be avoided. The sickness prevalent at this season has no doubt accentuated the precautions.

The festival has nothing spectacular about it. Its high antiquity and the fact that it is prescribed in the Book of Rites make it generally observed. According to this work the son of Heaven prepared himself for the ceremonies of this day by the practice of abstinence. On this day he led his high officials in an offering to Yen Ti, the cosmic deity of the south, which belonged to summer and fire. South of the capital on his return, he distributed rewards and granted apanages to feudal princes.

During the Han dynasty (206 B.C.–A.D. 221) the high officials dressed in red, made an offering to Yen Ti seven li south of the capital at a shrine seven feet high and on an altar of two terraces. They rode in red chariots adorned with crimson ornaments and equipped with long spears intended to assist the *yin* principle in its struggles. The ceremonies consisted of an offering and a ritual with evolutions performed by companies of eight men accompanied by the beating of drums. The number seven was sacred to fire and the even numbers represented the *yin* principle. In the Sui dynasty (A.D. 581–618) a temple was built to Yen Ti on the sacred mountain Hui Chi in Chekiang. The following dynasties continued offerings at this mountain and south of the capital with various modifications.

The festival is observed to-day among the people of Foochow by offering pancakes of rice flour, chopped vegetables and meat to the ancestors and the household gods. The cakes are presented to friends and relatives and eaten while sitting on the doorstep, or in the rice-mill. In this way they hope to avoid the evils of the season and attract the good. The onions and bamboo shoots in the cakes are said to aid eyesight.

The vendors of pork-stalls present beggars and lepers with a few pork-balls on this day. This not only wards off future disease, but prevents these gentry from surrounding the stall in large numbers and making business with ordinary people impossible.

In Kiangsu province the people beg wheat of their neighbours for their meal. They say that this releases summer sickness.

This is also the day when fashion prescribes that summer clothing be donned. In former days and even to-day this is still supposed to have a magical influence upon nature, but ere long it will be a matter of fashion entirely.

A large number of precautions are taken to keep disease away. In Yünnan province branches of the *tsao* tree are stuck in the doors to keep out calamities sent by demons. The people scatter ashes at the foot of walks in order to ward off snakes.

A large number of things are taboo : sitting on the doorstep because it produces weak feet, taking a siesta because it produces lassitude, and working the cattle because this will make them weary during the strenuous days of summer.

This being the first day of summer naturally determines the weather for the whole season. Various methods are employed to discover the future. If there is a halo about the sun there will be much rain. A north wind means much sickness. A south wind means in certain places a good catch by the fishermen. If the day coincides with the first day of the month there will be earthquakes.

The festival is not considered to be an important one, but its roots reach back to antiquity and the psychological uncertainty which pervades the atmosphere will continue to increase the sales of patent medicines whose advertisements occupy a large space in Chinese newspapers.

CHAPTER XXI

THE DRAGON BOAT FESTIVAL

The dragon boat festival is the popular name for one of the most generally observed and picturesque festivals in China. Like other seasonal celebrations its purpose was the harmonizing of the male and female principle in nature. The *yang*, or male principle, attains its culmination just before the summer solstice, and the *yin*, or female principle, comes into being and waxes until the winter solstice. The two principles are supposed to be in violent strife. Man's part is not only to stand by as a spectator, but to assist nature in this process and thus to help bring about normal conditions. Incidentally he must also use various methods to protect himself and his interests. The Chinese call the festival *tuan wu*, "the precise point of resistance," or *tuan yang*, "the culmination of the *yang*." Another name is "the heaven middle festival". These names express the ideas of the struggle between the two principles of nature.

The customs of this festival of the fifth day of the fifth month may be divided into those performed in the home and those which take place outside of the home. On the fifth day early in the morning every householder fastens on each side of the main door of the house a small bouquet of sweet-flag and mugwort tied with a red paper band. These plants are supposed to be picked with their roots before daylight. Their strong odour, which represents the male principle, is able to resist disease and spectres which proceed from the female principle. On the lintel are pasted powerful charms to ward off evil. Those with the stamp of Chang T'ien Shih, the so-called Taoist Pope, used to be the most efficacious. A common charm is that with the picture of the Thunder god wielding his lightning weapon. Another represents a monk with a mosquito brush by means of which he is able to sweep away disease and noxious vapours. Many people paste five coloured slips of paper with charms on them. The black colour represents the north, the red south, the blue east, the white west, and yellow the centre. The popular story tells of the five spirits of poison who descend upon the earth at this time and scatter their destructive vapours. The charms are defensive means against them.

These charms made of paper four inches wide and eight inches long are printed from blocks and sold on the streets for a few cash. In certain wards the caretaker of the local temple supplies his constituency with these weapons against the spirit world. Such charms are also placed over the bed. After a few weeks they are taken down and burned. The ashes are mixed with water and the concoction is given to children who have stomach trouble.

About twelve o'clock an offering is made before the ancestral tablets. The food is left before the ancestors for a while and then eaten by the members of the family. A prominent dish consists of three-cornered dumplings made of glutinous rice wrapped in bamboo leaves. These, with rice, peanuts, dates, and other fruits, resemble the *yin* and *yang* as they enfold each other.

During the day various prophylactic operations are performed. The house is carefully purified by the burning of sulphur squibs in the corners, under the beds and about the legs of chairs. This is said to remove snakes also. A liquid made of sweet-flag root and sulphur is poured into the wells. It is also used in washing the body. The noses and ears of children are smeared with it in order to counteract the poisons of insects.

On this day the children are provided with an apron with pictures of tigers and five poisonous insects painted upon it. These are the snake, the spider, the lizzard, the centipede, and the green frog. In the summer this is the only garment worn by small children and is not only useful because of the pictures painted on it, but because it protects the abdomen from chills.

Children and adults protect themselves against disease by various charms. Little bags filled with substances giving forth a strong odour are hung from the buttons of the coat. Charms made in the shape of tigers, frogs, the eight diagrams, watches, deer, peaches, an abbreviated calendar, and many other shapes deemed to have defensive powers against spirits are worn on the person. Even campholene balls are hung about the neck. The calendar containing the orthodox order of heaven as determined by the emperor was a powerful resister of evil under the dynasty. The peach, which blossoms early in the spring, contains a special amount of the *yang*, and so can overcome demons and give long life. The tiger is famous for his ability to gulp down evil spectres. An individual covered with such defensive armour is proof against disease so far as suggestion can make him so. The fact that these methods give confidence has perpetuated their popularity.

The fundamental principle of proper conduct is action in

accordance with nature, which means that one's whole life should be attuned to the various seasons of the year. The Book of Rites gives directions for conduct during this time of the year which have been followed by the scholars and officials and have exerted a great influence upon the social life of the people. The Book of Rites says : " This is the month when the day is longest. The *yin* and the *yang* struggle together. Life and death are in conflict. The superior man practises abstinence inward and outward. He retires within his house. He must not be hasty. He avoids all things which excite the ears and stir up the sexual passion. He partakes lightly of delicacies and must not take highly seasoned foods. He controls his appetites. He quiets his heart and spirits. The officials reduce their business. They do not inflict severe punishment. In this way they assist the female principle in nature (*yin*) to exert its proper influence." This practice has been followed for so many years that it has become second nature. The officials do not inflict capital punishment. Under the dynasty they reduced the number of blows upon culprits. Many abstain from eating meat, so much so that the meat stands find business somewhat dull.

The day is surrounded with all sorts of taboos also, some of which are very sensible. People are advised not to abide in damp places, not to expose their body to the light of the moon and stars during this period. The moon is the embodiment of the *yin* principle and hence moonlight may convey disease. Nor should inquiries be made after sick people at this time inasmuch as such curiosity stimulates the demons of sickness to activity.

Presents expressing the felicitations of the season are

exchanged. The bride's family present summer clothing, three-cornered dumplings and a fan to the newly married bride. The custom of presenting fans with appropriate sentiments indited upon them is ascribed to the Emperor T'ai Tsung of the T'ang dynasty (A.D. 627–50) who made presents of fans with beautiful sentiments written upon them so that as the air was set in motion the virtue of the people might be increased.

The customs performed outside of the home are numerous and important. Herbs and plants picked upon the morning of the fifth day of the fifth month have great curative value. Behind this is a theory that nature provides a remedy for every ill and that the greater the ill the greater the efficacy of remedies—on the whole a very optimistic view of nature. The medical works of China abound with recipes made on this day. One from the holy man Sun from the seventh century A.D. is still used to-day. "Take the moss from the tile roof, or ashes of many plants, add salt and mix with water. This is good to rinse the mouth with. Boil Szechuan pepper in vinegar. This will cure all kinds of teeth troubles."

The great Materia Medica of the Ming dynasty among its 1892 different medicines contains this: "On the fifth day of the fifth month pick a hundred kinds of herbs, dry by exposing to the air, burn, mix with lime, make a paste, bake, and then reduce to powder. Smear this over wounds to stop the flow of blood. Plaster over bites of dogs. Mix with fresh water, make a dough, heat till it becomes white, add sharp vinegar, and make into small cakes. Take a cake under each armpit and squeeze. When the cakes are dry change. This treatment will take away general pain and stop eruptions.

Wash eruptions with urine. After three washings the eruptions will heal."

Another recipe from this thesaurus is as follows: " On the fifth day of the fifth month about the noon hour, if it is raining, quickly split a bamboo. In the bamboo will be found a powerful liquid. Use it to cure heart and stomach troubles and to keep the vital spirits from congealing and collecting. It will also cure worm troubles. Mix with otter's liver and make into tablets. This taken internally will drive away fever, destroy phlegm, will quiet fears and soothe the spirit."

Another formula advises: " Take water from a wheel rut, or from the imprint of a cow's hoof to wash scrofula on the neck and to cure rheumatism."

These various customs are intended to assist nature to make a happy transition over this period and also to protect man from the many diseases which are common during this time of the year. But that does not account for all that is done at these festivals. Some of these magic ceremonies have taken on characteristics of play by which high tension is reduced and a critical situation in man's life happily passed.

CHAPTER XXII
DRAGON BOAT RACES

The dragon boat races form a picturesque feature of the fifth month festival in parts of China where the floods have been troublesome. In other parts there are horse races and other contests which have the same purpose, namely, the assisting of the processes of nature.

Near the city of Foochow in south China every village located near a stream or body of water owns a dragon boat. This is a narrow boat 40 to 60 feet in length with both prow and stern curved upward. On the prow is a dragon's head with whiskers and fins. The sides of the boat are painted to resemble the body of this mythical animal. In northern Hunan where these races originated boats are said to be from 75 to 115 feet long carrying a complement of from 40 to 80 men. In Foochow the boats carry 28 to 36 men.

Each boat is under the command of a captain selected by a local committee for his daring as a sailor and his ability as a fighter. Quite frequently an aquatic victory must be confirmed by success in a fistic contest on shore. The captain selects his crew from the boat people. He with his mate stands in the prow of the boat. In the centre is a drummer and one who beats time on a gong to keep the rowers together. On the stern stands the steersman wielding an oar twenty feet long by means of which he can swing the boat about quickly. The rowers seated on each side propel the boat by the rapid strokes of their paddles.

During the year the boat is stored in a long low shed against the village temple. In the fourth month the committee

DRAGON BOATS.

connected with the temple call upon each householder and collect the regular contribution. Often this is done by the boat-women who go from shop to shop carrying a shallow bamboo tray with the flag representing the boat and accompanied by the drummer and the beater of the gong.

Towards the end of the fourth month the boat is pulled out from the shed, the spiders and their cobwebs swept out and necessary repairs are made. The crew begins to practise in their leisure hours.

Before the boat is launched proper precautions are taken to appease the spirits so that they will not interfere with victory. Near Changsha, Hunan, an offering of food and wine is prepared. An exorcist performs somersaults from prow to stern, scatters buckwheat and purifies the boat by fire, while the drums and gongs are beaten to frighten away the evil spirits. On the day of the races when the rowers have taken their places he lights a small quantity of oil. If the flame flares up high it means victory. If the blaze is dim and low it means defeat. But even such an ill omen may be overcome by the use of powerful spells whose names are sufficient to terrify any demon. He employs such spells as " Stopping the soldiers of *yin* ", or " Causing the mountains to be moved into the sea ", or " Savage Thunder ". He repeats :

" Heaven's fire the bright sun burns.
   Earth's fire the earth to ashes turns,
   But when Thunder's flame flashes far and wide
   The evil demons quickly hide.
   By Thunder's flame now purified
   The boat may o'er the four seas ride."

When the boat is in the middle of the stream as a final precaution the exorcist brushes out the evil influences with a wisp of grass. The boatmen throw a peach and a pot of rice and beans into the water, an offering to the water spirits. Similar ceremonies are observed wherever dragon boat races are held.

Each boat is under the protection of a guardian deity. A village near Foochow, Wo Siong, had the monkey god as the protector of its boat. Often the image of the guardian god is carved on the prow of the boat. Quite generally these gods are the spirits of men who were drowned under some peculiar circumstances.

The races present a picturesque spectacle. The long narrow dragon-like boats with the dusky, half-naked rowers, the spray cast up by the glistening paddles, the rythmic motion responding to gong and drum—these once seen are not soon forgotten. The races are rather informal affairs since the starting point and goal are not clearly defined. There are no starters and no judges. In fact it would be impossible to find men brave enough to assume these positions. There is a general understanding, however, that when a boat gets ahead of another and keeps its place it is the winner. The contest is one of the hit or miss go-as-you-please affairs in which all may come off as victors in some respects.

These elastic rules add to the interest of the contests to the Chinese and also give occasion to many tricks and disputes. Each boat manœuvres for a good position in the middle of the stream. A common ruse is to roll up the flag and cease beating the gong and drum and thus pretend to quit the race. When the opponents are off their guard, however, the boat starts up and gains an advantage. Another trick is to wait around until a race can be negotiated with a crew tired out by its previous races. A common trick is to lift the heavy steering oar out of the water and thus lighten the boat. Handicaps, figured in boat-lengths are given, after prolonged negotiations.

The uncertainties of the contest, the promise of a good feast and the opportunities for an interesting fight attract the younger element who are bored by the deadly monotony and drabness of village life. Every year a number of people are drowned and some are killed or injured in the fights which decide the final victory. The official records abound with eloquent proclamations against the festival and its evils, but the festival is as popular as ever. This is especially the case after a severe drought, or flood which are usually ascribed to the laxness in holding the races.

When the races are over an offering is prepared. The exorcist recites a spell over it.

"As the dark waters down the river flow
  So may all maladies, diseases, plagues, and death with it go."

This done, the flag is furled, the boat with drum and gong silent is rowed to the shore and is placed in the shed near the temple.

The races would not be complete without a bountiful feast and presents to the participants. The feast takes place in the temple of the guardian god. There are usually two bowls of the different kinds of food for each one and the bowls are extra large. Among the presents the fan occupies a conspicuous place. Thus concludes the festival auspiciously begun with a feast in the temple of the guardian god in which the gods and men are brought in harmony and understanding at the critical time of the summer solstice.

If we ask a Chinese scholar about the origin of the races, he will refer to the history of Sze-ma Ch'ien, the Herodotus of China, who tells about Ch'ü Yüan, a privy counsellor of the prince Huai of the state of Ts'u about 314 B.C. This official was a very efficient man held in high esteem by his prince. One day the prince ordered him to draw up certain regulations. A rival desired to obtain a copy of these regulations before their publication. This the counsellor refused. Whereupon the opponent piqued by the refusal denounced Ch'ü Yüan to the prince. The prince became angry and estranged. Ch'ü Yüan became sad and distressed. He first tried to console himself by composing a poem entitled "The Dissipation of Sorrow". In this he doubts not only the justice in the present world, but also seems to be uncertain as to any compensation in a future world. In this depressed state of mind he clasped a stone to his breast and jumped into the Mi Lo River in northern Hunan. Thus far the historical record. The commentary adds that this took place on the fifth day of the fifth month and that the people of Ts'u observed the day yearly by racing with dragon boats and casting offerings of rice into the river in memory of the day when fishermen sought for the body of the privy counsellor.

This is not the only story explaining the festival. Another legend tells of a maiden, Ts'ao O, whose father, a wizard by profession, was drowned on the fifth day of the fifth month about 180 B.C. Inasmuch as the body could not be found, the daughter, then fourteen years old, wandered along the bank of the river and finally threw herself into the water. After a few days her body rose to the surface and in her arms she clasped the body of her father. This occurred in Shaoshing in Chekiang.

Undoubtedly other sections of China have a legend explaining this festival. It is hardly probable that the suicide of a disappointed counsellor, or the exhibition of filial piety on the part of a daughter would produce such a widely observed festival. The counsellor appeals to no patriotic feeling. He was merely an unfortunate man and of such there have been many in China. Still his name is attached to the festival, but in a different capacity from a disappointed politician and dreamy poet.

Ch'ü Yüan and others who have met a watery grave are regarded by the people as powerful deities who control the waters and who may send them down in destructive floods which devastate the countryside and destroy human life, or they may dispense them as fructifying and beneficent rains bringing bountiful harvests and prosperity. These spirits are associated with the Dragon Lords whose sway over the floods is supreme. The races and the offerings are intended to propitiate these supernatural beings. In different parts of China other methods are used, but the purpose is the same. In certain parts of the Chihli province on the fifth day of the fifth month during a drought the women wash sieves on the river bank and pray for rain. In certain parts of Shansi a sacrifice is made to the dragon lord and idol paper money is offered on the gardens and fields. In the Loochoo Islands just off the coast of China the people make a special offering to the spirit presiding over rice. In Foochow the people say that the races bring great peace, which means good harvests and an absence of disease.

Thus all over China the time of the festival is regarded as a critical period in nature. The various customs and the boat races allay the disturbed minds of the people, stimulate hope and make for unity and relieve the strain and monotony of life. More and more the magic element is falling into the background and the play and festive aspects are coming to the front.

CHAPTER XXIII
THE DRAGON

The dragon is one of the most ancient and widely known beings in China. In fact he may be called omnipresent. Whether it be in art, religion, social life, or politics he has occupied and still occupies an important place. The emperor's throne was called the "dragon's throne". His countenance was the "dragon's countenance". When the emperor died he ascended "the dragon throne on high". The top of the ancestral tablet is a dragon's head. The bridal robe is embroidered with dragons. Then there are the dragon boat festival and the dragon lanterns. Buddhists still pray for rain to the Dragon Kings. The dragon idea has intertwined itself into all phases of social and political life and embodied itself in art and finds expression in literature.

The dragon is a mythological being. There is no question that the first impulse to the development was given by the large beasts who roamed over central Asia and who left behind their immense carcasses preserved in stone. It may be that a part of them synchronized with early man. But if they did not, the huge fossils found in caves in different parts of China were sufficient in a superstitious age to start the idea of this mythical beast.

Whatever the origin of the idea may have been, popular fancy has played a great part in constructing the image of this animal deity. He started with a well-known animal belonging to the saurians who at one time roamed over Asia. Quite early he was drawn with the head of a horse and the body of a snake with wings on its side. At about the Christian era the dragon was regarded as composed of the parts of nine animals. He had the horns of the deer, the head of the camel, the eyes of the devil, the neck of a snake, the abdomen of a large cockle, the scales of the carp, the claws of the eagle, the soles of the tiger, and the ears of an ox. The dragon also possessed the virtues of all these animals.

The dragon being divine was possessed of many powers, among which the ability to change itself at will, or by a process of evolution, was prominent. An old record says: "The small dragon is like a silk caterpillar. The large dragon fills heaven and earth. When it arises, it gallops over the clouds. When it hibernates, it crouches in the abyss. According to one theory the scaly dragon becomes a dragon in a thousand years. In five hundred years more he becomes a horned dragon and in a thousand years more he becomes a flying dragon."

Quite early the dragon became linked up with the constellation of Virgo, the Balances, and the Scorpion. The star Spica is the head of the dragon. In the early days it seemed as though the dragon was following the sun and so always the dragon has before him a globe which represents the sun.

Buddhism further humanized the dragon by making him a dragon king. The Chinese at the present day in their prayer for rain address the dragon king whose image does not resemble a dragon at all but is like a human being.

What are the functions of dragons? The dragon from early times was associated with rain and storms. As such he has been regarded as a benevolent being who brings prosperity and fertility and happiness to the world. In this respect the Chinese tradition about the dragon differs from Ahriman of the Persians, or the dragon as pictured in the Christian tradition where he has been regarded as a malevolent being. This does not mean that harm is not connected with the dragon at some time. The violent typhoons, and the destructive rains which accompany them as well as earthquakes, have been regarded as visitations by the dragon along the coasts of China. On the whole, however, the ordinary phenomena of storm and rain have dominated the conception. In the dry season the dragon is supposed to hibernate. In the rainy season he ascends up into the sky and sends down rain.

The dragon has from time immemorial been connected with the imperial throne. In several ancient records it is stated that a great emperor was born after the queen stepped upon a dragon's footprint, or was enveloped in a cloud. The phrase " to mount the six dragons " means to be an emperor. " The dragon flying in the sky " means the approach of a new sovereign.

Not only emperors, but great men are connected with dragons. There is a story about a visit of Confucius to Lao Tzu, the founder of Taoism. Confucius reports to his pupils : " Birds I know are able to fly, fish I know are able to swim, beasts are able to walk. Those who walk we catch by traps, those who swim we capture by nets, and those who fly we overtake with arrows. But as to the dragon, I do not know how he mounts the wind and clouds and thus ascends to heaven. I have seen Lao Tzu to-day. Is he not like the dragon ? "

The dragon has been the medium of revelation in ancient

China. The records speak of the dragon writing, which came up from the river. The great men were always associated with dragons from whom they derived their wisdom.

The dragon has not only been a religious and social power, but its bones, teeth, and saliva have been employed as medicine. A writer of the sixth century states that these remains of the dragon were found in large quantities in Shansi, especially in the valleys and precipices of T'ai Shan. Szechuan, Shensi, Hunan, Chekiang and Hupeh are also mentioned as places where these fossils were found. There is no question that the fossils passed off as dragon bones are the remains of animals found in caves and on the banks of rivers. The Chinese classify them in various ways. The horns are the most efficacious. The bones from the head and back are considered good, especially if they have a white base. If the bones stick to the tongue when licked they are considered genuine. The bones with small veins belong to the female and those with coarse lines belong to the male.

These fossils are sold as medicine in the shops. The bones cost about one-twentieth of a cent for ten candareens. The teeth are more expensive, retailing at the rate of one-half a cent for ten candareens. The saliva is most expensive, costing twenty cents for one candareen. A careful examination by experts has revealed that these bones belonged to the rhinoceros tichorhinus, mastodon, elephas, equus et hippotheria.

These fossils are prepared in various ways. A very powerful medicine is made by boiling them with a fragrant grass, then washing twice, reducing to powder and hanging in a silk bag with a young swallow after its entrails have been taken out above a well. The list of ills cured by such concoctions makes a patent medicine advertisement seem genuine. An introductory list of diseases cured contains the heart and stomach troubled by devils, hiccoughs, dysentery, bloody pus, women's diseases, obstruction of bowels, children's fevers and convulsions. Another list included hate, anger, ulcers, and paralysis.

The dragon has a large place in Chinese art. Flags with dragons embroidered upon them were used by the ancient Chinese in their worship of Heaven. Quite early images of the dragon were employed in the prayers for rain. Jade was carved in the form of the male and female dragon. The dragon is intertwined in painting and architecture. In literature he is celebrated in song and verse.

From ancient times the dragon was worshipped. Wang Ch'ung speaks of the worship of a clay image of the dragon in the second century B.C. Buddhism introduced the Dragon Kings of the five directions. The Chinese regard the centre as the fifth direction. These dragons were given the title of king in A.D. 1110. A little later the dragon mother was recognized with titles.

The Manchu dynasty continued the offerings inaugurated by previous dynasties. In time of severe drought the officials prepared an offering to the dragon king. First, the slaughter of animals was prohibited for three days. If this had no effect upon the weather an offering was made at the temples of the Dragon Kings and at the altars of the gods of the grain and ground. The prayer spoken on the occasion introduces us to the heart of the ceremony: "This year, month, day, N.N. official offers sacrifice to the spirit of the dragon king having the imperial title of 'Conferring blessing on the Ming country (Fukien) assisting and prayer answering'. The god's power overflows and encircles the ocean. It fertilizes and waters all living beings. It ensures and brings about the tranquillity of water and land, causing the streams to follow their courses. It enlarges and helps the water springs to be useful. It sends the fertilizing rain at the proper time. He tranquillizes the billows. He holds in his grasp the benefit of the great water streams. His great merit produces joy in all things. All beings look up to and trust the spirit's gift of prosperity and protection. We make our thanks and offer bountifully and carefully observe all regulations. Together on a lucky day we spread the feast and respectfully arrange the sacrificial animals and silk."

In time of prolonged drought the people make an image of the dragon king consisting of a bamboo frame covered with yellow paper or cloth. The head is that of a dragon, the body resembles that of a man. This is placed over a man or boy and carried in procession accompanied by the beating of drums and gongs. A line of men and boys carry flags with the words "The rain is coming", "Let it rain". One man with two buckets of water on a pole across his shoulder dips a willow branch in the water and sprinkles the road crying out, " The rain comes, the rain comes." After parading about the town they come to the office of the magistrate who bows and offers incense before the image.

In certain places during seasons of extreme drought a piece of iron is put into a pool of the black dragon. This is connected with an old theory that certain elements produce and create each other. The dragon being during drought under the influence of heat will make liquid of the metal and thus produce rain.

Thus through the ages the dragon has embodied the ideals of the Chinese. His pre-eminence has received a little set back during the revolution. No doubt more and more he will occupy the place in legend and story and amuse future generations of children.

CHAPTER XXIV

MOTHER EARTH

The worship of Mother Earth was common to all the nations of antiquity in Asia and Europe. In Babylonia she was known as Ishtar and was taken over into the religion of Canaan as Ashtoreth. The Greeks according to the Iliad sacrificed a black sheep to Ge, the all-producing and all-nourishing mother. It is not surprising, therefore, to find this goddess worshipped in China from ancient times.

Mother Earth is designated in the Shu Ching as Hou T'u, which means sovereign or goddess earth. Usually her name occurs with that of August Heaven in the phrase August Heaven and Sovereign Earth. She is also called Hou T'u Ch'i, meaning the female deity of earth. In the Shu Ching the name Hou T'u occurs but once. In the year A.D. 5 Wang Mang, in order to further his schemes of usurping the throne, gave the goddess Earth the title of "Sovereign Spirit of August Earth", and raised her worship to the same level as that given to Heaven. He had given his daughter to the weak emperor P'ing Ti in marriage and hoped in this way to raise her dignity and incidentally his own. During the Sung dynasty in the reign of Huei Tsung (A.D. 1101–26) she was given the title of "Tutelary Spirit of Sovereign Ground and August Earth obediently following Heaven's laws, of great virtue and very illustrious"!

Having considered the names and titles of goddess Earth, let us look at the origin of the conception. The famous commentator C'hing K'ang-ching of the Han dynasty said that the goddess of earth was located in the Kunlun mountains of Tibet. These mountains rising to a height of twenty thousand feet and covered with eternal snows form the backbone of the continent of Asia. In them rise the mighty rivers which water the great plains of China. About their base spreads out on four sides the great continent of Asia and this in turn is bounded by the four seas. The conception of the world as square surrounded by four seas with the high Kunlun range occupying the centre and dominating all is no doubt a very ancient one. Another commentator of the Han dynasty calls the plain to the south-east of the Kunlun range Shen Chou, the isles of the Shen, and within this is China itself. This plain also had a sovereign goddess who ruled over all matters subject of course to the goddess in the Kunlun mountains. From early times the goddess of earth was connected with the Kunlun mountains and the great plain called Shen Chou. These two names occur in the rituals of the different dynasties. The common people have anthropomorphized the goddess and regard her as the wife of the god of wealth. In fact this connection with the Kunlun mountains is not thought of in many parts of China.

Distinction should be made between goddess Earth and the tutelary gods of the ground and grain. Goddess Earth rules over the whole country. The tutelary gods of the ground and grain are local. Their rule is bounded by the village, the district, the country, the province.

From earliest times the goddess Earth was worshipped on a square altar placed in shallow water or surrounded by a moat with water. The square terraces, being two or four in number, represented the earth, and the moat represented the four seas. The colour of the altar was yellow, being the colour of earth. It was usually in the northern suburb of the capital. The Han dynasty had its capital at Ch'angan (Sian Fu in Shensi). The Kunlun range was north-west of this. The north is also associated with the female principle to which earth belongs.

In the Han dynasty there was a famous temple to goddess Earth on the river Fen Yin north of a place called K'uei Ch'iu. Here the emperor Wu Ti built a fine temple and near it five altars to represent the five directions. Here there was an image of the goddess. This worship at this place was continued more or less regularly by all the dynasties up to the Yüan dynasty. Since the time of this dynasty it has fallen into desuetude.

The altar to goddess Earth of the Ching dynasty was located outside of the northern wall of Peking. The grounds about it are spacious and planted with trees. In 1860, when Peking was captured by the French and English armies there was plenty of room for the two armies. On the grounds are various buildings used on the occasion of the sacrifice. The altar consists of two terraces reached by two flights of stone steps each about six feet high. The terraces are faced with yellow glazed brick. The altar is surrounded by a deep ditch and by walls. The two innermost walls are yellow.

The time of worship of goddess Earth from earliest days has been at the summer solstice early in the morning. At this time the *yin* principle is born and begins to wax strong. The *yang* principle begins to wane in power. It is therefore in accordance with the Tao to sacrifice to earth at this time. There have been departures from this at different times.

During the Han dynasty several emperors sacrificed to earth in the third month. This date corresponds to the time when nature is born. The worship at the summer solstice was made to the goddess in the Kunlun mountains. The goddess of Shen Chou was worshipped sometimes in the summer and in some dynasties in the first month of winter.

From early times the Chinese have associated departed emperors and empresses with goddess Earth. The tablet, or image of earth occupied the second terrace on the altar and those associated with it were arranged on either side according to their rank. In the year A.D. 50 the empress Lu Hou, the wife of Kao Tsu, the founder of the Han dynasty, was associated in the worship of goddess Earth. But since the character of this empress was very disreputable she was deposed in the year A.D. 50 and Po Ki, a concubine of Kao Tsu, and the mother of Wen Ti (179–156 B.C.) was put into her place on the altar. The Wei dynasty, A.D. 220–64, adopted the queen of Shun (2255–2205 B.C.). During the T'ang dynasty the emperor T'ai Tsung (A.D. 627–50) was associated with earth. The last dynasty associated all its ancestors from T'ai Tsu Kao Huang Ti (1616) onward.

On the terrace below were the tablets of the five sacred mountains, the five guardian mountains, the four great rivers and the four seas and also the famous mountains of the emperor's own country. This arrangement probably obtained from early times.

The worship of earth by the emperor, or his proxy has varied in its details from dynasty to dynasty. It will be impossible to enumerate the changes made in the offerings and in the ceremony. The great purpose was to conform to the supposed nature of earth and in this way persuade Mother Earth to grant the blessings which the people desired. The emperor, or his proxy represented the people on this occasion as pontifex maximus. A prayer used on this occasion will interpret the sacrifice. "Thou fertile Earth, assisting the spirit of Heaven, producing the balmy wind and sweet rain. All vegetation, all the grains thou dost produce in great abundance. Now that we are quiet and at peace I, N.N. reverently worship the powerful spirit of lower earth." The offerings repeat concretely the same prayer to the all nourishing mother.

Not only was sacrifice made to earth at the summer solstice and other stated times, but from remote times important events were duly reported to it. In the Book of Records we read the announcement made by T'ang (1766–1753 B.C.): "Therefore, I, little child, charged with the decree of Heaven and its bright terrors, did not dare to forgive the criminal. I presumed to use a dark coloured victim, and making clear announcement to Supreme Heaven and Powerful Earth requested leave to deal with the ruler of Hsia as a criminal." In the Chou Li we read: "Whenever the king granted an oppanage he announced the same to Goddess Earth." This custom has been followed to the present day. That the Republic will not do away with it altogether is quite evident from the fact that the military governor of Fukien announced his victory over the Imperial forces to the tablet of Confucius and the provisional president of the republic made a similar announcement at the Ming Tombs in Nanking.

In the popular religion the earth has been humanized. She is the wife of the god of wealth and is worshipped on the second day of the second month. Still, the wider significance is retained in many parts of China. In Foochow the people prepare a gruel of glutinous rice, sugar, dates, peanuts, beans, water-chestnuts, loquats, and white almonds. Early in the morning a table is placed in the main reception room of the house on the edge of the open court with an incense burner, candles, and three bowls of this gruel. The head of the house takes three sticks of incense, lights them and after holding before his forehead reverently places them in the burner. Then he kneels before the table and bows three times. Firecrackers are let off and idol paper is burned. The table before the ancestral tablets and the tables before the other household gods contain ten bowls of this gruel.

The married daughter presents a bowl of the gruel with one dish or four dishes of condiments. The seeds in the broth represent a good harvest and prosperity. The presenting of the gruel by the daughter is an attempt to influence Mother Earth to remember the aged and to regard with favour the filial piety of the young and bestow upon them a bountiful harvest. Year by year these eloquent prayers are uttered by the Chinese and Mother Earth has certainly smiled upon them through the centuries. For, they are possessing the land and are accomplishing the most important thing in the struggle for existence, namely, managing to exist through several thousand years.

CHAPTER XXV
THE SUMMER SOLSTICE

The festival of the summer solstice does not possess the characteristics of a popular festival. This is no doubt due to the fact that its place has been taken by the festival of the fifth month, fifth day, the so-called dragon-boat festival. Whatever customs are now performed are fossilized remnants of former ages.

In Foochow the festival passes by without any public expression. About six families out of ten make a thin dough out of rice flour and pour it upon the sides of the heated rice cooker. Before it forms a dry crust it is scraped into the bottom of the cooker. Meat and vegetables are added and the mixture is eaten for breakfast. This dish is prepared at other times of the year, but on this day it has attached to it a new significance, namely, that those who eat it will promote their health and happiness and prosperity and avoid sickness and trouble.

In Kutien, near Foochow, the work of sowing the fields is now ended. The husbandmen make an offering of candles, incense and food to the gods of the ground either before a tablet or in the open field. After the offering the family enjoy a feast together.

This simple festival has been observed in different ages and different parts of China from the dawn of civilization. It is based upon views of nature which have formed the foundation of religion and morals. The Chinese believe that the sun, moon and stars, in other words the visible firmament revolves around the earth. This revolution produces the twenty-four seasons, the eight seasons, the four seasons, the hours of the day, the succession of day and night. It does more, it produces the vapours or the forces which are active during these divisions of time. This revolution of the visible heavens is called the Tao. According to a more refined and abstract conception the Tao is the reason and the intelligence which is behind the revolution and its outward results. The Tao manifests itself through the interaction of two principles, the *yin* associated with cold, darkness, and death, and the *yang* associated with warmth, light, and life. The *yang* is born at the winter solstice and increases until the summer solstice. With it comes spring and all its blessings. At the summer solstice the *yang* attains its growth. At this time the *yin* is born. It struggles with the *yang* for mastery and overcomes. In its wake follow ripeness, decay, and death. It produces demons and spectres and noxious vapours. The *yin* belongs to the element water. On the other hand the *yang* belongs to fire. These two elements influence and are influenced by the other three elements, wood, earth, and metal in various ways. The element water produces the element wood. Fire destroys wood. Metal produces water. When we realize that all things are dominated by one or more elements which determine their nature and that these elements interact upon each other and that this interaction is either promoted or hindered by the *yang* and *yin* principles we have the main principles which underlie the customs and activities and divinations at this season of the year.

The Chinese have employed various methods to determine the day of the summer solstice. In the book of Records we read, "The day is longest, the constellation is that of fire (stars in the azure dragon). By this the second month of summer is correctly determined." In very early times the day was fixed by more primitive methods. We see a survival of this in the Tso Chuan where an officer in charge of ceremonies connected with the summer solstice is given the name of a bird which began to sing at the summer solstice and stopped at the winter solstice. By the time of the Han dynasty the shadow of the gnomon was measured. In the Han Books we read : "The sun occupies the light pathway. At the summer solstice it comes to the north of the stars of Gemini near the pole. Therefore the shadow of the gnomon is short. Place a standard eight feet high and the shadow of the gnomon will be one foot five inches and eight-tenths." This method has been employed almost to the present time.

From very early times down to the present the day of the summer solstice was celebrated by the rulers of China by an offering to Mother Earth. The Chou Li says: "The instruments of music were played at the square altar in order to call out the spirit of earth so that it might be worshipped." The altar was square to resemble the shape of the earth. It was surrounded by water. The musical instruments were such as to harmonize with the supposed nature of earth. This sacrifice by the rulers recognized the sovereignty of earth over its products. It gives birth, nourishes and completes. It blesses mankind. The offering was a prayer to obtain the blessings of Mother Earth and avoid its displeasure and punishment. This sacrifice changed somewhat in outward form in different dynasties, but its purpose has ever been the same. During the Han dynasty the worship took place once in three years in a temple to Mother Earth. In other dynasties it took place every year in the northern suburb of the capital.

Not only did the rulers observe the day, but the superior man and the people all tried to adapt their conduct so as to be in harmony with the season of the year. The Li Chi says: "This is the month when the longest day comes. *Yin* and *yang* strive together. Death and life are separated. The superior man performs abstinence inward and outward. When he is resting he should certainly have his body covered. He should not be hasty. He should give up music and sexual intercourse. He should not go out visiting. He should reduce rich foods. He should not disturb the harmony of vapours. He should curb his desires. He should establish the vapours of his heart. The hundred officials cease public business. They do not execute punishment. Thereby they determine and put to rest that which the *yin* principle has completed." These principles have been followed. The popular mind has extended them and made them more concrete.

The Feng Su T'ung I (the latter part of the second century) says: "At the summer solstice put on five coloured threads and escape evil produced by the powers of the *yin*. Write the characters *yao kuang*. *Yao kuang* are fierce demons. If you know their name you will not have pestilence and disease." The Wu Ching says: "At the summer solstice the *yin* begins to stir, but it has not yet pervaded everything. Therefore weapons are not to be moved and drums are not to be beaten. Public business is not to be begun. By this the minute vapours are assisted in their growth.

The popular customs have elaborated these principles in a concrete way. In the history of Kiangnan we read that in the district of Kiating situated in Kiangsu province, " at the summer solstice take cocoons, beans, and wheat boiling into a porridge. It is called the summer solstice porridge. Do not sit in the doorway. K'ang says, he who disobeys this rule will catch the summer sickness. Three hours after the summer solstice you should not wash, should not take manure out to the fields, do not scold, curse, or utter imprecations. It is said that the god of heaven descends among men. If it is clear on this day the heat will not be great."

In Chekiang province in Haining the people sacrifice to their ancestors. In Shaoshing, " At the summer solstice the farmers of the mountains gather together. They have contests with boats. They dress up small children, and sing folk songs. They take ten men into one boat and race up and down. The onlookers are like a wall." At Tungyang in the same province " At the summer solstice all who till the fields whether many or few prepare wine and meat to offer to the spirit of the ground and grain. They tie grass together in the shape of an idol, place it on a standard in the field and make an offering to it. This is an offering to the goddess of the fields. For though the wheat harvest is bountiful and the grain is luxuriant the purpose of this offering is to pray for blessings and make a thank-offering."

At the summer solstice certain things should be avoided. The work Tsun Sheng Pa Chien written during the Ming dynasty says : " In the latter part of the night of the summer solstice the universal *yin* is born. One should take hot things. Also he should take hot liquid medicine for building up the kidneys." It goes on further, " after the summer solstice it is necessary to dig the well deeper and change the water in order to ward off pestilence and sickness."

Predictions about the weather are made at this time. In the books of the Sui dynasty (A.D. 581–618) we read : " The day of the summer solstice belongs to the thirtieth diagram *li*. Those who desire to prognosticate regarding the future should watch at noon for a red cloud resembling a horse in the south. This is the *li* vapour coming and is favourable to millet. If the *li* vapour does not come, the sun and moon will not give their light, the five grains will not ripen, men will be sick with eye troubles. In the winter there will be no ice corresponding to the same time in the eleventh month. If a wind follows the *li* there will be a bountiful harvest."

In Chihli in the district of Suning " On the day of the summer solstice if the wind comes from the east many people will be sick. If the wind comes from the south, it is called a favourable wind. It will be very warm. If the wind comes from the west, there will be great rains in the autumn. If the wind comes from the north, the water will come down from the mountains ".

In these ways the Chinese have sought to bring themselves into harmony with nature and so obtain its blessings and ward off evils.

CHAPTER XXVI
THE RULER OF EARTH

According to Taoist philosophy there are three primordial powers, namely, heaven, earth, and water each presided over by a tutelary deity. The Chinese also recognize three important periods in the year during which these deities rule. The first period is that of the birth of nature in the spring controlled by the Ruler of Heaven whose festival is celebrated on the fifteenth of the first month by a great display of lanterns. The second period begins at the end of summer or the first month of autumn when nature begins to ripen controlled by the Ruler of Earth whose festival is celebrated on the fifteenth of the seventh month. The third period is that in which the powers of dissolution and death dominate. It begins with the first month of winter, namely, the tenth month and is controlled by the Ruler of Water whose festival is celebrated on the fifteenth day of the tenth month.

The festival to the Ruler of Earth culminates on the fifteenth of the seventh month though it may be celebrated a few days earlier. In the course of its long history it has centred about the duties of caring for the old, worshipping the ancestors and providing for the wandering spirits.

The usual offering to the ancestors is enlarged by the addition of quantities of idol paper money, paper with pictures of warm garments and other articles required by the departed in view of the coming of winter. These packages of picture clothing are marked with the name of the person for whom they are intended. More elaborate offerings include

SHRINE TO GENERAL WARD AT SUNKIANG
(Illustrating the deification of an American soldier).

houses made of a bamboo frame covered with paper with paper servants and sedans with bearers. These are consigned with due ceremony to the flames and thus transferred for the use of the dead. In ancient times these articles were buried with the dead. In the neolithic hearths recently excavated in various parts of north China we find the objects with which the living was surrounded buried with him. These also included wives and slaves.

The provision for the wandering spirits has formed an important part of Chinese religion. Under the dynasty a regular State offering to these abandoned spirits in each provincial capital, prefecture, chou and district was performed by the magistrate or his proxy. The prayer or rather announcement made on this occasion gives a very clear idea of the purpose of the offering. It is as follows: " All people who dwell under heaven and on sovereign earth have a doctrine about spectres and souls. Although Hades is separated from the world of men, still the laws of the two places are similar. Just as there are regulations governing the treatment of living men so there are regulations for worshipping the spirits of the departed. It should be remembered that in the realm of shades there are spirits to whom no offerings are made. Formerly these spirits were living men and it is not known how they died. Among them are those who died of wounds in battle. There are those who died on water, in fire, or were killed by thieves. Some were killed while they were robbing men. Others were killed in the act of abducting men's wives and concubines. Some met their death by judgment, although they had committed no crime. There were those who died by disease sent by Heaven. Some were killed by ravenous beasts and poisonous insects. Some died of hunger and cold. Some died in personal combats. Some succumbed to dangers. Some died because a wall fell on them. Some who died left no children. These orphaned souls without anyone to supply their wants are worthy of great pity. They lurk in the grass, or are attached to wood. Some of them cause strange phenomena, or monstrosities. Some cause strange apparitions. They wander to and fro under the light of the stars and the moon calling piteously in the wind and rain.

"To-day we meet the exalted spirits and preside at this sacrifice respectfully placing the altar west of the city. In the month (first, seventh, or tenth) on the happy occasion we respectfully prepare animals, food, broth, and rice for the purpose of sacrificing to all the spirits to whom no one sacrifices in this whole district or prefecture.

"You spirits should all know this and come to enjoy the offering. If in all this district there are unfilial persons causing disturbance, ridiculing the law, imposing upon good persons, if there are any malicious, unorthodox, bad characters, ye spirits will report them to the city guardian, revealing their deeds so that they may come before the officials. If their crimes are slight, they will be beaten with a bamboo or a rod. If their offences are serious they will be punished by being made slaves, by banishment, or they will be hung, or their heads will be cut off. In case their offences are not revealed, then let them meet their punishment in Hades, or may their households meet death by dire calamity.

"If there are those who are filial, peaceful, law abiding, doing good, straightforward, ye spirits will report them to the city guardian. He will assist them secretly, causing their families to be at peace and their farming to be successful. He will enable their fathers and mothers, wives and children to be a protection to their neighbours.

"If among us officials there are those who impose upon the dynasty above and oppress the good people below coveting riches, practising fraud, destroying the government like a worm does books, injuring the people, ye spirits will not oppress the whole body of officials, but will clearly reveal the culprits. If you do this way then the matters will be thoroughly investigated. We officials do not offer a flattering sacrifice. May you enjoy the offering."

The abandoned souls of the dead are remembered on this occasion by the people. The offering to them is made in the evening on the street before the main door of the house. Candles and incense are stuck into the ground. A platter with small dumplings and cakes is placed on the ground. The head of the house comes out, kneels and bows three times. A large quantity of idol paper and paper with pictures of clothing is burned before the door. A few of the dumplings are thrown into the street. A beggar comes along and picks them up. Large shops and wealthy householders make a more pretentious offering. A platform with three tiers is erected in the shop, or in the main reception room of the house. On the top tier are placed an incense burner, candles, cups with wine, large bowls with dumplings made out of rice flour and brown sugar. There may be ten, twenty, or thirty of these bowls. Each bowl should have forty-nine dumplings. This is the number of days required for the services of the dead for the purpose of rescuing them from Hades.

When the offering is ready, three Taoist priests take their

position on the second tier. The middle one is called the head of the tier or throne. In his hand he holds an ivory tablet which resembles that held by idols and the ministers of state of ancient times when they were in the presence of the emperor. On the first tier there are five priests. The priests repeat their incantations accompanied by ringing of bells, the beating of drums, and the rattle of clappers. At twelve o'clock the ceremony stops. The powers of the lower regions hold sway till twelve o'clock when the rule of the powers of light begins. Large quantities of idol paper and paper with pictures of clothing are burned. The next morning the food is divided among the neighbours.

The Chinese believe that these abandoned souls spread skin disease among the children. Many of these spirits were beggars, lepers, and vagabonds during their existence on earth, and this class of people has various skin diseases. The sedan coolies make offerings to these spirits so that they would not trip the coolies when they are carrying sedans.

In all these ceremonies the Ruler of Earth seems to have been forgotten. This is practically so. The main thing is to keep these abandoned souls from injuring men. In the popular mind the Ruler of Earth is a very shadowy being. Still in the incantations of the Taoist priests the Ruler of Earth holds a prominent place. The following passage from the sutra which is repeated at the festival by Taoist priests will relate the different ceremonies together and make clear the position of the Ruler of Earth in the Taoist theology.

"Thou art in the palace of the northern capital, beside the azure grotto of the gods. Thy board has forty-two departments; all together there are ninety million people. Thou rulest over the three regions, the ten directions, the whole world. Thou dost control the five guardian mountains, the eight poles, the four corners of the earth. Thou dost let out and take in the *yin* and the *yang*. Thou dost examine the records of men and women. Thou dost mercifully nourish heaven and earth. Thou dost examine the names of all beings who should receive punishment and blessing. The fountain of thy laws and methods is vast, being able to rescue a man from the nine dark places. During the vast kalpas (long ages) thou dost hang up lights and so art able to remove ten thousand sins. Thou art the father and mother of all living beings. Dead and living receive thy favour. Great art thou in kindness, great in favour, the great holy one, the great merciful one."

The ripening and the decay of vegetation and the coming on of winter suggested to the ancient Chinese that the spirits of the departed and the abandoned souls roaming about were in need of nourishment and they made offerings to them so as to make them contented and prevent them from doing injury to men. This is the heart of the festival to-day just as it was long years before the Christian era.

CHAPTER XXVII
THE GOD OF WAR

Kuan Yü, usually called the god of war but actually the god of sincerity and loyalty, was a general in that picturesque period of Chinese history known as the Three Kingdoms (A.D. 221–65). He is an example of the process of deification common in China.

The Han dynasty, founded by Liu Pang, the prince of Han, a feudal state bounded on the north by Shensi and on the east by Honan, being the territory near the river Han, was drawing to its end. It is the most famous dynasty of China. The Chinese still call themselves "the sons of Han". Their language is the "Han language". Shih Huang-ti, the First Emperor (246–209 B.C.) was able to conquer the semi-independent feudal states which comprised China, but he was unable to weld them together into an empire. This task the Han dynasty accomplished with wonderful success. With this purpose in view it improved internal communications by building roads, bridges, and canals. It extended the borders to include Kwangtung, Fukien, Yünnan, Szechuan, and Liaotung. It opened intercourse with India and the Roman Empire. Its great work, however, was the unification of Chinese culture. It collected the classics and engraved them on stone to provide a standard text. It fixed the penal code now being superseded by modern law. It organized the literary examinations abolished in 1905. It made Confucianism a State religion. Under its leadership China became the great nation of Asia.

The Han dynasty finished its work and was succeeded by the Three Kingdoms. The Wei ruled the central and northern provinces with Loyang as its capital for fifty years. The Wu dynasty ruled what is now Hunan, Hupeh, Kiangsu, and Chekiang with its capital at Nanking for forty-six years. The third, which was the real successor to the Han dynasty, the Shu, ruled over Szechuan with its capital at Ch'engtu for forty-four years. Its founder was Chao Lieh Ti (221–3) called also Liu Pei, kinsman of the reigning family of the Han dynasty.

These Three Kingdoms entered upon a contest for supremacy. Chao Lieh Ti with his faithful general Kuan Yü, the present god of war, attacked Wu and was defeated. His son (A.D. 223–58) united with the Wu dynasty against the Wei dynasty. They were defeated by Sze-ma Chao, the general-in-chief of the Wei troops. The latter was succeeded by his son Sze-ma Yen (A.D. 265) who founded the new dynasty of the Western Tsin which gave a semblance of unity to China from A.D. 265 to 290, and put an end to the Three Kingdoms.

Kuan Yü was born at Chieh Chou in Shansi in the second century of our era. According to tradition he was a seller of bean-curd, but applied himself to study. Very early he cast his lot with Liu Pei, called Lieh Ti above, taking an oath of allegiance in a peach orchard which has become a model for future generations. At first Liu Pei defended the Han dynasty, but when this collapsed he attempted to carve out an empire for himself.

The records agree in praising the bravery, but above all the loyalty of Kuan Yü. In one of his many battles he was hit by an arrow in the arm. Although the wound healed he felt much pain in the arm during damp, rainy weather. His physician said that the poison of the arrow had penetrated the bone and that it was necessary to make an incision and scrape the poison from the bone. Kuan Yü invited his friends to a feast and while feasting and joking had his arm cut.

His loyalty and courage are united with a resourcefulness which has always been admired by the business men of China. In A.D. 200 Ts'ao Ts'ao, the founder of the Wei, took Kuan Yü prisoner. He tried by various ways to alienate him from his master and win him to himself. One night he put the doughty warrior into the same room with the two wives of Liu Pei. Our hero stood in the ante-chamber all night with a lantern, thus saving the reputation of the ladies. Ts'ao Ts'ao also heaped titles upon him, but all to no purpose.

Still Kuan Yü was not unmindful of these favours, and desired to show his appreciation of his former enemy. The opportunity came when Ts'ao Ts'ao was engaged in a battle with Yu Liang. When the armies were in battle array with Yu Liang in the centre of his army, Kuan Yü whipped up his horse, dashed forward, cut off Yu Liang's head and brought it to his chief. Then he returned all the kind letters sent him by Ts'ao Ts'ao and went back to Liu Pei, his first master.

The above is a brief story of the earthly career of our hero. Kuan Yü's last military operations took place in Kingmen Chou in the central part of Hupeh. It was here that he laid down his life for his master and here he was buried in a mountain called Yü Ch'üan, Jade stream, near the city of Kingmen. The memories of his fidelity and heroism were kept alive in this neighbourhood. In the year A.D. 260, forty years after his death, he was given a posthumous title by Hou Chu, the son of Liu Pei, of "Brave Virtuous Marquis". In the year A.D. 583 during the Sui dynasty he was given the title of "Sincere and Merciful Duke".

Up to this point his posthumous history is like that of many another hero. The years rolled by. In the T'ang dynasty in the year A.D. 676, the emperor Kao Tsung built a monastery to the six Buddhist Patriarchs in the mountain of Yü Ch'üan, and Kuan Yü, whose grave was not far away, was made a tutelary god of the place, that is, he was charged with the defence of Buddha, the law, and the community from the maras, the spirits of darkness, the enemies of universal order. In this way he gradually took the place of the Indian god, Indra.

From this monastery his fame rapidly spread to other monasteries in China, for the monks are great travellers and propagandists. His power against the demons was soon acknowledged by the Taoist pope and the people of China. From the time that he was recognized as the great adversary of the demon world his future as a god was assured.

His subsequent history is easily told. According to the local history of Chieh Chow, Kuan Yü's birthplace, his temple in Chieh Chou was repaired by imperial order in A.D. 1008–17. In the year A.D. 1096 a tablet was presented to the temple of Kuan Yü at Yü Ch'üan, with the title of "Prayer Answering Illustrious King". In A.D. 1108 he was given the title of "Brave Peace Bringing King". In 1129 the emperor Kao Tsung granted him the title of "Brave, Virtuous, Righteous, Warlike King", and regular official sacrifice was made to him.

According to the regulations of the Ming dynasty during the reign of Chia Ching (1522–67) the thirteenth day of the fifth month was fixed as the birthday of the god of war. The actual birthday is on the twenty-fourth of the sixth month, but the regard for the father does not permit the celebration of the birthday after that of the son which occurred on the thirteenth of the fifth month. An offering was made to him consisting of one ox, one goat, one pig, five kinds of fruit, and one roll of white paper representing silk by the president of the board of worship. All important events were announced to the god of war. In 1614, in the reign of Wan Li of the Ming dynasty, the god of war was granted the title " The great Ti subduing the demons of the three regions, Heaven exalted one whose powerful authority makes the most remote stand in awe of him, Kuan the holy ruler". The minister of the Board of Rites presented the god with a crown of nine pendants (the emperor has twelve pendants, the marquis has nine), also a belt with gems, a dragon garment, and a gilt tablet with the above title.

The Ts'in dynasty added further titles. In 1856, because of his assistance in the Taiping rebellion he was made the equal of Confucius. His temple is found in Peking, and in the capital of every province, prefecture, chou, and district. In all there were about 1,600 official temples. Besides these numerous other temples were supported by the community. The temples to the god of war may be found in all parts of the world wherever there are Chinese. There are usually two other images found with that of Kuan Ti. One is that of his son Kuan P'ing who was faithful to him till death ; the other is that of Chou Ts'ang, a devoted companion.

The official sacrifice to Kuan Ti took place in the second month and the eighth month, and on the thirteenth day of the fifth month. In the first month the thirteenth day a special offering is also made to him.

On the days of the official worship the temple was swept. Before the image of Kuan Ti were placed an ox, a goat, a pig, dishes of fruits and rolls of white paper representing silk. Candles were lighted and large sticks of incense sent up their fumes. The old musical instruments were brought out and the children of the local school performed military evolutions with plumes. Before daylight of the appointed day the officials gathered with their retinue and together knelt thrice and performed three bows at each kneeling. When the worship was over the meat of the sacrifice was divided among the participants. Besides these stated days incense was burned on the fifteenth day of each month.

The god of war is very popular among the people, and especially among the merchants. On his birthday, which among the people of Foochow is celebrated on the twenty-fourth day of the sixth month, meats of various kinds, candles and incense are spread before the image of the god. Idol paper is burned and firecrackers are let off. The head man performs the bows for the rest. When the sacrifice is over the clerks of the shop enjoy a bountiful feast upon the food presented to the god. We can readily see why he is popular with the merchants. His great qualities are loyalty, courage, justice, and generosity. The Chinese merchant has similar qualities. He is loyal to the members of his guild, he is bold in his ventures, he has a keen sense of justice and above all he is noted for his generosity. Of course the god's power over demons and spectres is responsible for a great share of his popularity. We shall speak of this later.

Kuan Ti is also one of the gods of literature in which rôle he is represented with a copy of the Spring and Autumn Annals, which he was able to repeat from beginning to end. This work is one of the classics of China which used to be employed in the State examinations.

Perhaps we ask what has made Kuan Ti so popular among all classes of people. The explanation is not far to seek. He is popular because of his supposed power over demons. When he was given the place of Indra during the T'ang dynasty his popularity was assured. The great occupation of the Chinese was the destruction of demons and Kuan Ti was supposed to be one of the most efficient destroyers of the powers of darkness.

Here is one instance taken from many found in the History of Kuan Ti. At Chieh Chou, the birthplace of Kuan Ti, during the Sung dynasty in the reign of Ta Chung Hsiang Fu (A.D. 1008–17) the salt springs which brought large revenues to the central government diminished their supply of salt. An official was sent by the throne to investigate the springs. The official reported that in a dream he saw an old man who called himself the god of the walls and moats. This old man told the official that Ch'ih Yu, a rebel against authority subdued by Hwangti (2697–2597 B.C.), was troubling the springs. The spirit of this ancient rebel was sent by Shangti the god of heaven to guard the springs. The emperor had set up a temple to Huangti, the sworn enemy of Ch'ih Yu, near the springs. On this account Ch'ih Yu had decreased the amount of salt in the springs. Ch'ih Yu sent a message by the god of the walls and moats to the effect that if the temple of Hwangti was removed he would stop troubling the springs. If this was not done he would bring greater calamity. This was a very serious matter, and so the Taoist Pope was sent for. He burned charms and recited incantations and requested Kuan Ti, the god of war, to drive away the evil spirit. Kuan Ti with sword in his hand promised to do so. Soon after this there was a terrific storm at Chieh Chou. The heaven was darkened. The air was filled with the clang of weapons and the stamping of horses. When the skies cleared the springs gave forth their salt as of old. As a reward for this service the temple of Kuan Ti was repaired and sacrifice was made in it.

There is quite an old work which was revealed in a dream in the monastery of Yü Ch'üan mountain in Hupeh, the place where Kuan Yü was buried. It is called T'ao Yuan Ming Sheng Ching, namely, The Canon of the Illustrious Sage of the Peach Orchard. This work had many obscure places and so it was explained in a dream by the god Wang T'ien Kung in the year 1810. My copy was printed in Foochow City in 1884. We shall understand the place of Kuan Ti in the people's life from a passage in this work. The following are the blessings which he confers on men. "No disease can touch the man who copies and prints this book. The family which respects this book, will find that things of ill omen and demon brutes turn into dust. The boat which honours this book will find that rough waves will become calm. The traveller who carries this book with him will have a safe and peaceful journey. The scholar who reads this book will soon become famous. The woman who repeats this book will bear two girls and five boys in her family. If it is repeated in behalf of the dead, they will quickly pass through hell and be reborn into this life. If it is repeated in behalf of father and mother, they will live to an old age. If it is repeated daily three, or five times, or if it is repeated many times all the gods will be joyful. The house and home will be illustrious, the evil will turn to luck. The blessing, imperial favour, and longevity will be increased."

The book leaves the reader in no doubtful state of mind as to how this is to be accomplished. All the gods, the tutelary deities of the five mountains, the god of thunder and lightning, the gods of the five lakes, and the spirits of the four seas, the gods of the sun, moon, the great dipper, the twenty-eight mansions of the moon, the god of the walls and moats obey the order of the exalted Lao Tzu, the head of the Taoist pantheon. These employ the tutelary gods of the ground, the tutelary spirits of the year, the month, the day, the hour, the runners in charge of the dark malignant influences, the pure white soldiers in charge of the day, the ancestors, the god of the hearth. These investigate, report, and bring reward.

We shall close with an order of worship taken from the same work. "Set up an image of Kuan Ti. If an image is not convenient then in the middle of a large sheet of yellow paper write the words, "Kuan the holy emperor the great demon subduer Ti". On his left place Chang Hsien T'ien Chün, on his right place Ling Kuan T'ien Chün. (Both of these are popular divinities.)

"Make offerings before them in the centre of the room. Practise abstinence, wash, put on clean garments, light a pair of candles, present three sticks of lighted incense, tea, wine, and fresh fruit. Kneel respectfully three times and bow the head nine times. When this is complete then repeat three times while kneeling, " The Precious Revelation of Wang Ling Kuan." Then continue kneeling and repeat three times " The Precious Revelation of Kuan the Sage Emperor ". Then repeat once the True Sutra revealed by the divining pen. Then arise, rest a moment, lift up purified incense twice and arouse your whole soul. Then kneeling repeat " The Canon of the Illustrious Sage of the Peach Orchard ". Then bow the head and arise. Rest a moment and quiet your spirit. If your body is weak and you feel weary, repeat the canon standing up, with hands clasped together. When you come to the phrase, " The sage's name," kneel and bow once and so manifest your respect. This is permissible.

" The important thing is not repeating much or little, but repeating with a sincere heart. It is more profitable to repeat at night. At night the most profitable time is before daylight, the first part of the fifth watch. At this time man's vital spirit is very strong. All nature is quiet. The spirit is not vexed and troubled.

There should be also decorated candles and pure incense. The lights should burn brightly. The heart should be unified and the mind should be fixed. At this time the repeating will have great effect.

" The canon should be wrapped carefully in a clean cloth. It should be placed high up. The women and children should not be allowed to touch it. Before repeating the hands should be washed."

During the presidency of Yuan Shih-kai, Kuan Ti was

exalted to a high position. All generals and soldiers had to take an oath of allegiance to Yuan before the image of this deity associated with Yüeh Fei, another hero of the Sung dynasty. Since then he has been quite prominent in the army.

CHAPTER XXVIII

THE WEAVER AND THE HERDSMAN

The festival of the seventh day of the seventh month embodies in ceremonial and story the aspirations, the hopes, and the fears of the maid and of the young married woman. The story is told that after the weaver and the herdsman were married they enjoyed each other's company too much and neglected their several duties and so the Lord of Heaven, the father of the weaver, separated the couple, placing one on one side of the Milky Way and one on the other side. Throughout the long year the two are parted, but on this night the magpies make a bridge across the Milky Way and the couple meet for a little while. Their parting is usually followed by a light shower.

The weaver is identified with Vega and two stars of Lyra and the herdsman consists of three stars of the constellation of Aquila. In the northern parts of China, where this festival originated, the seventh month marked the end of the harvest and the cessation of outside work for the women who turned their attention toward spinning and weaving. As they sat on the doorsteps of their huts plying their handcrafts the bright Vega sent its bright bluish beams upon them. She became the patron of the spinners and of the weavers. Just across the Milky Way was the lonely swain longing for his love. The motive of the story is supplied from the agelong struggle of youth between duty and pleasure.

The festival has been celebrated from time immemorial.

The spinning maiden as the patroness of woman's work and as the one who rules over melons, fruits, silk, and the gathering and storing of precious things has been the chief object of worship. The herdsman has simply a decorative and hortatory value, though in certain parts of China this day is regarded as the bull's birthday. Branches and flowers are hung from the bull's horns and the cowboys are presented with vermicelli and cakes.

In Foochow the women make a special offering to the spinning maiden consisting of seven bowls of various kinds of melons, seven bowls of food, the usual candles, incense and idol paper. Frequently on a table near by are placed needles, thread, scissors, and other articles used by women in their work. After the incense has been kindled and each of the women has bowed thrice, the idol paper money is lighted and while it flickers the women try to thread seven needles. Their skill is judged by the number they succeed in threading. In some localities they put a spider in a box, and if he makes a web, this is regarded as a promise of skill in weaving and sewing.

All over China the offering is accompanied by various methods of stimulating skill in woman's work. In parts of Chihli province melons are cut up so as to resemble a flower with petals. On the petals are placed needles. These are offered on a platter to the spinning maiden. They are then laid aside for awhile and if a spider weaves a web in them it is regarded as a sign that the women of the house will become skilful with the needle.

In the province of Shansi the women place wheat and bean sprouts in a jar of water. If the shadow of the sprouts are pointed it means that the women will be deft with their fingers. If the shadows are indistinct it means the contrary.

In the province of Honan a white cloud over the Milky Way during the offering is regarded as evidence of blessing for the women of the house.

In Foochow a method of discovering whether a wife has been untrue to her husband is employed to this day. A house lizard is killed, dried, and made into powder. This is mixed with water and when rubbed on the woman's body produces various shapes. Then powdered cinnabar is rubbed over the body. If the cinnabar remains on the body the woman has not been guilty of adultery. If the cinnabar colour disappears, then she has been guilty.

Medicines compounded of herbs picked on this day have special efficacy. Hemp flowers dried and made into powder and soaked in hempseed oil will prevent the hair from falling from the eyebrows. Lily roots boiled and made into powder will produce black hair when rubbed on the spot from which the white hair has been pulled. If the children swallow seven beans they will be kept in health during the year. A wart rubbed with seven melon leaves by the patient who faces south in the north room of the house, will disappear.

The festival and the legend have been celebrated in poetry, of which the following is a good example :—

> Brightly shines the Starry River
> Flowing down the Heavenly glade ;
> From the north-west comes the " Herd-boy ",
> From the south-east looks the " Maid ".

Quickly waves a white hand shapely,
Sadly smiles her beauteous face,
When she sees her faithful lover
Far across the glittering space.

Arms stretched out towards each other,
With impulsive feet they stand,
Eyes with sorrow's tears bedewed
On the Star-Stream's shining strand.

But, alas, that bridgeless River
Is the cause of all their pain,
Dooming "Spinning-Maid" and "Herd-Boy"
Nevermore to meet again.

    By Luh-ki. Chinese Poems, Charles Budd.

CHAPTER XXIX

THE HARVEST FESTIVAL

The harvest festival, celebrated from the eleventh to the fifteenth of the eighth month, is one of the most joyous occasions of the year. The harvest is assured and a part of it is already gathered in. The sunshine is bright and the air bracing with just a tang of cold. The harvest moon, the consort of Heaven, rises large and smiling and bathes the festivities with its mellow light. While thanksgiving is in the background of this occasion, the dominant note is the enjoyment of Heaven's bounty and the sharing of it with gods and men.

The moon occupies the central place in the various ceremonies. Such expressions as "pursuing" or "congratulating" or "rewarding" the moon indicate the important place of the moon. The moon is associated with the harvest and is also the abode of the immortals and therefore the symbol of the mysterious force which controls life and death and the future. Both of these motives have gathered about themselves the symbols in art and story, and find expression in many of the customs.

The observances in Foochow illustrate the varied customs in China. The ancestors are especially remembered on this occasion with a bountiful offering. An offering is also presented to the household gods and particularly to the "mother", a goddess who protects children. An elaborate offering is also made to the "seven star mother" who dwells in the constellation of the Great Bear. A four sided rice measure with some rice in the bottom is placed on a table in the front of the reception room or in the open court. In it are put ten pairs of chopsticks and images which represent the children of the family. These are about six inches to a foot high, often consisting of a stick of wood with the features painted on it. If the child dies they are placed in the coffin. After the age of sixteen these images are discarded. If the family is in good circumstances a priest is invited to recite incantations. At a certain point in the ceremony the head of the family and the children kneel and worship before this altar. This will prevent them from succumbing to disease, and will ensure long life. Congee made of the rice in the bottom of the measure prolongs life.

The wealthy families and shops set up altars in the courtyards, or in front of their establishments consisting of several terraces. On the top terrace they place a pagoda and incense burner. The other terraces are occupied by the eighteen Buddhist Arhats, the eight Taoist Immortals, cassia flowers, and other decorations which are supposed to be characteristic of the palaces of the moon. Elaborate ceremonies are conducted by Taoist, or Buddhist priests.

On the fifteenth and several nights preceding the two pagodas of Foochow are decorated with hundreds of lanterns. On the night of the fourteenth thousands of men and women go to the tops of three hills in Foochow and there offer incense in a large iron urn to Heaven and Earth, the father and mother of the people.

The festival is a joyous occasion for the children. The bakeries and candy shops exhale sweetness and beauty. Each district boasts of possessing the secret of producing the large round moon-cakes made of flour and brown sugar and decorated with likenesses of the moon and its palaces. The toy shops abound with small pagodas and animals done in clay capable of moving head or limbs and producing curious noises when squeezed. On the streets the children build pagodas with bits of tile. Many of these pagodas are never finished and so the common proverb applied to people who begin things and do not finish them is that they are building tile pagodas.

The night of the fifteenth is the high point of the festival. Tables are spread in the courtyard, or upon the open platforms on the roofs. It is believed that beautiful flowers fall from the moon at this time and that the women who see them will be blessed with numerous progeny and the men with prosperity. The feasting continues long into the night. The scholars compose poetry. Music and games add to the merriment.

Similar to other great festivals this is also a time of settlement of outstanding accounts. The creditors present the bills and expect payment of at least one-half. The rest is allowed to go over until the great settlement at the end of the year.

Numerous devices are employed to get light upon various problems of life at this time. The women place a cloth over a basket, or a vessel and as the moon rises they invite the goddess of the moon to come down. After they utter their prayer they listen for noises. An even number of raps means a favourable answer while an odd number indicates a negative answer.

Various prognostications are made about future weather.

If the moon is hidden by clouds, then on the Lantern Festival of the following year there will be snow. If the moon is hidden the whole year will be empty and void.

The festival has been celebrated in verse and story and legends pieced together from little scraps from different ages and different parts of Asia are the common possession of the people.

LEGENDS ABOUT THE MOON. JOURNEYS TO THE MOON

There are various records about journeys to the moon which surpass the wonders of the airplane. The best known are those of the emperor Ming Huang of the T'ang dynasty who died A.D. 762. The Lung Ch'eng Lu written about the twelfth century contains this story: "The emperor and the Taoist pope and a Taoist doctor made a journey to the moon on a cloud. They found the moon cold and the fog made their clothes wet. On the moon they saw a crystal field ten thousand *li* in extent over which immortals and Taoist doctors were riding back and forth on clouds and cranes. They beheld also more than ten thousand goddesses of the moon in white garments mounted on white phœnixes who were dancing and gambolling on the hills under the cassia trees. The emperor heard most ravishing music. The following night he wanted to go again, but the Taoist pope would not go."

BRINGING DOWN THE MOON

One of the favourite tricks of the Taoist doctors was that of bringing down the moon. According to the work Hsüan Shih Chih written during the T'ang dynasty a certain scholar said to his guests: "I am able to cut off the moon and place it into my sleeve." He commanded them to leave the room and tied together several hundred chopsticks and mounted them saying, " I am about to climb up and take the moon." Then the room was darkened. Then he opened the room and said that the moon was under the dress of one of the guests. Out of the fold of the dress there came out a moon over an inch in diameter. Then suddenly the whole house was very bright and the cold penetrated the muscles and the bones. This story is no doubt the reproduction of impressions made upon simple minds by a stereopticon simply constructed. The moon an inch in diameter is the ray of this lantern projected into the folds of the garments by an accomplice in the dark room.

The Rabbit in the Moon

The tradition that there is a rabbit in the moon is old in China. Ch'ü Yüan, the counsellor of the prince of Huai (328–298 B.C.) in his Dissipation of Sorrow says : " By the virtue of what power does the light of the night die and come to life again ? This property is only due to the rabbit in its bosom." The philosopher and critic Wang Ch'ung (A.D. 19–90) discusses the tradition of the rabbit and the frog in the moon and comes to the conclusion that these animals do not exist there. On the other hand Chang Heng (A.D. 78–139) in his work on astronomy says : " The moon is the nucleus of the vital essence of the *yin*. When it is gathered together it produces the forms of animals. The rabbit belongs to the *yin* since its number is even." There is an old tradition that the rabbits in the earth are all females, and that they conceive by gazing at the rabbit in the moon and vomit the young from the mouth.

The following story about the rabbit in the moon was made popular by the Hsi Yu Chi published in A.D. 646: "At the beginning of the ages there were a fox, a monkey, and a hare. Although they were of different species, they were happy together. One day the god of heaven transformed himself into an old man and came to the three animals asking for food. Thereupon the fox brought a carp and the monkey brought fruit to the old man, but the hare returned empty-handed. He was distressed at his weakness and ignorance, and so threw himself into the fire in order to complete the repast of the old man. The old man took the roasted hare and sighed and said to the fox and the monkey: "I am moved by his devotion and will not destroy his name in the world." Accordingly he sent him to the moon. This was repeated by succeeding generations. Hence arose the story about the hare in the moon."

Later Taoist tradition relates that the hare in the moon is pounding drugs in a mortar out of which the immortals make the elixir of life.

The Man in the Moon

The man in the moon is called Yüeh Lao and has been considered as the matchmaker in marriages. According to ancient Chinese tradition, "Matches are made in heaven, and the bond of fate is forecast from the moon." The story is told of Wei Ku who saw in the town of Sung an old man sitting in the moonlight and turning the leaves of a book. In response to his inquiry the old man informed him that the volume contained the matrimonial destinies of all mankind. Thereupon the old man took a red cord from his wallet saying: "With this cord I tie together the feet of husband and wife. Though born in hostile households, or countries widely separated their fate is inevitably fulfilled at last. Your wife, I will tell you, is the daughter of an old woman named Ch'en, who sells vegetables in yonder shop." Having heard this Wei Ku decided to investigate and saw a woman carrying about an ugly child about two years old. He was so displeased that he hired an assassin to kill the girl. The man dealt the blow, but did not kill the girl. Only a small scar above the eyebrow remained to mark the foiled attempt. Fourteen years later Wei Ku was married to a beautiful girl. A few days after the nuptials, he noticed a patch of gold leaf upon her eyebrow. After insistent inquiry she said: "Your maiden is the adopted child of the prefect. My father died in Sung city. While I was young and was carried in the arms of my nurse, a thief struck me. The scar is still there."

To-day the go-between who arranges the marriage is called Yüeh Lao, though she is usually a woman. At the engagement contracts are exchanged. The young man's is called *yang*, the name for the male principle, the woman's is *yin*, the female principle. In this contract there are two needles joined by a red thread. At the marriage ceremony the newly joined couple drink wine from two cups joined together by a red cord. So from time immemorial the old man in the moon has tied the bonds between husband and wife with his red cord, and thus added his compulsion when the will to love grew weak.

The Goddess of the Moon

The Chinese have not only a man in the moon, but also a goddess of the moon, Ch'ang O or Heng O. In the Land and

Water Classic a story is told as follows:—" In the great desert there is an elevation called the sun and moon mountain. It is the axle on which the heaven turns. At Wu Chi, the gate of Heaven, where the sun and moon enter, there is a spirit without arms. The two legs are joined to the head. The mountain is called Hsü. There are maidens who wash the moon. When the wife of Ti Chun, Ch'ang Hsi, gave birth to twelve moons the young maidens began to wash them."

A story of the archer lord who lived in the twenty-fifth century B.C. is told by Chang Heng (A.D. 78–139) as follows: " Hou I received from the queen of the western paradise the elixir of life. His wife, Ch'ang O, filched it and ran away to the moon. But before she departed she went to a diviner, Yu Huang, who assured her that her journey would be attended by good fortune, saying:—

> " Young wife, swiftly fly away
> And to the western moon thee safely hie
> Through gloom and darkness never fear
> For future ages will thee glorify."

So Ch'ang O went to the moon and there became a striped toad."

After Ch'ang O left her husband pined for her day and night until he became ill. A lad came to see him on the fourteenth of the first month at evening, and said: " I am the messenger of your wife who knows of your longing for her. She is unable to come back. But to-morrow when the moon is full place round cakes resembling the moon on the north-west side of the house and call the name of your wife. She will come down three evenings." He followed the lad's advice and at the appointed time met his wife.

SOLVING THE ETERNAL PROBLEM "WILL HE LOVE ME?"

The Frog in the Moon

We have already seen how the frog came into the moon according to popular tradition. The philosophical tradition from early times connected the moon with water. The Yih Ching, often called the Bible of the Chinese, states that the "Kang diagram is water and is the moon". Huai-nan Tzu (d. 122 B.C.) says: "The congealing of the cold vapours of *yin* becomes water. The essence of the vapours of water becomes the moon."

The moon being the essence of water controls water. Its connection with the tides was noted very early. It was also regarded as producing rain. The Shu Ching says, "The course of the moon among the stars produces wind and rain."

But not only does the moon produce water, it controls all beings which live in water. Huai-nan Tzu says: "The moon is the source of *yin*. Therefore when the moon wanes, the brains of the fish contract. When the moon vanishes the univalves do not complete their growth." Again, "Bivalve shells, crabs, pearls, tortoises grow and contract with the waxing and waning of the moon." Lu Tzu says: "The moon is the origin of all *yin*. When the moon is full then the shells become full and all *yin* objects grow luxuriously. When the moon is dark, the shells are empty and all *yin* objects decrease. But when the moon is visible in the heavens, all *yin* objects are transformed in the abyss."

In Indian mythology the frogs are identified with the clouds and the croaking of the frogs represents thunder. When the frogs have been satisfied with plenty of rain they stop croaking. The moon is supposed to bring or announce the rain and so the frog associated with the rain clouds is also associated with the moon. This connection is further strengthened by the fact that the colours of the frog, green and yellow, are also present in the moon. It is quite possible that this Indian view found its way to China. This is further substantiated by the fact that the frog seems to be classified by the early Chinese with the insects rather than with the animals which live in water.

The Trees in the Moon

The Chinese mention at least eight different species of trees to be found in the moon. The most noted of these is the cassia which blossoms in the fall and gives out an exquisite perfume. Its beauty is celebrated in rhyme and story. The literary candidate who was successful at the examination was said to have " plucked a leaf from the cassia of the moon ".

The cassia has been regarded as possessing great medicinal powers. That which grew in the moon made the body immortal, transforming it into a pellucid crystal form which could fly upon the clouds and range through the universe.

During the Sung dynasty the *sala* tree, sacred in the memory of Sakyamuni's birth and death, was identified with the cassia. The story was related of Kang Wu, a man who aspired to become an immortal but sinned, and who was punished by being compelled to chop this tree. As soon as he made a cut, the tree closed up and he wasted his life away at this impossible task.

The seed of the cassia from the moon was brought to earth by a rooster of Yen Chou to the southern part of China. At different periods the seeds of the cassia fell to earth in large quantities like rain. Some were white, some yellow, and some black. The monks of a monastery at Hangchow planted them and obtained twenty-five trees. From these came all the plants of the cassia in China.

CHAPTER XXX
KITE FLYING

This festival, observed in various ways throughout eastern Asia, is known as the "double nine" because it comes on the ninth of the ninth month. It marks the coming of the autumn frosts and its purpose is to enable man to make an easy and safe transition to winter.

The story of the origin of the festival is found in an old work of the sixth century A.D. A certain famous sorcerer once warned his friend that a great calamity was impending over him and his family on the ninth day of the ninth month, and advised him to go up into the hills and hang small bags containing hellebore on the arms of the members of the family and dose them with aster wine. This the friend did. After their return to the house they found the chickens, cows, and goats dead about the court. Out of gratitude for this escape from death they kept the day ever afterward.

The story dramatizes the first killing frost which occurs about this time in north and central China where the festival originated.

The various customs were at one time prophylactic measures to ward off this deadening influence from men. In fact this motive is still operative to-day, though some of the activities have been sublimated and serve quite a different purpose. The aster wine and hellebore were popular because these plants were immune from the first frosts. The trip to the hills was regarded beneficial because the hills were not touched by frost as soon as the lowlands.

The festival was observed by the people living north of the Chinese outside of China proper. During the Liao dynasty (A.D. 907–1168) established in the Liaotung peninsula, the emperor held a special reception on this day and presented his officials with aster wine. The officials spent a part of the day shooting at an image of a tiger. Those who made few hits were compelled to give a feast to the company at which aster wine figured prominently. They also sprinkled powder made of hellebore on the doors in order to ward off evil. The Kin Tartars (A.D. 1115–1234) worshipped Heaven on this day.

At the present time the festival is noted for its kite flying in many parts of China. By the beginning of the seventh month the kites begin to appear in the shops and on the hills. As the day approaches the kites increase in number and variety. There are bird kites, round kites with squashes, sun and moon painted on them, box kites, kites with long tails and without tails. There are kites which give forth a weird sound as the wind passes through them. At night lanterns are suspended from them and the sky seems to be dotted with new stars. Old and young enjoy the sport together picnicking upon the hillsides. They vie with each other in making their kites fly as high as possible. Some try to hook their opponent and pull him down. The air resounds with shouting and laughter. The evening is spent in feasting at which the aster wine and the nine-layer cakes made of rice, flour, peanuts, and dates occupy a prominent place.

The kite flying has been enjoyed in China for many centuries. We are told that Mo Tzu, fourth and fifth centuries B.C., made a kite of wood and after experimenting for three years made it fly. Han Hsin (d. 196 B.C.), general of the founder of the Han dynasty, employed the kite to learn how long he would have to make his tunnel in order to undermine the palace of the city which he was besieging.

The custom of flying kites from the hills dates from the seventh century A.D. In this century the literary examinations were reorganized and the celebration of kite flying took place after the results of the examinations were announced.

The kite was imported to the West from China. The earliest mention of it in Europe is found in a French-English dictionary of 1690. The English word paper-kite is an exact translation of the Chinese word chih-yuan. The German "fliegender Drache" and the French "cerf-volant" suggest the Chinese origin.

CHAPTER XXXI
THE CITY GUARDIAN

The City Guardian, Ch'eng Huang, is the protector of the walls and moats of the city. His temples, found in every provincial capital and district city, were kept in good repair under the old regime. In recent years, however, they have been used as barracks by soldiers and have lost their former significance.

To the emperor Yao (2356–2255 B.C.) is attributed the honour of making the first offering to this god. At first the worship took place under the open sky, but quite early temples were built. As the cities increased in number and importance this god grew in popularity. In A.D. 934 he was granted the title of Prince. In the Yuan dynasty (A.D. 1206–1341) his spouse was granted a title of priestess. At the beginning of the Ming dynasty the official worship was performed on open altars, but later was transferred to the temples. Under the Manchu dynasty the god had the same rank as the highest official of the city in which the temple was located. The City Guardian was nominated by the Taoist pope for a period of three years and was subject to promotion, or removal thereafter. The candidates were deceased officials. Such power of nomination of deceased officials could have been turned toward political ends in a country where the people have long memories and strong loyalties to persons. To prevent such abuse the names of the candidates were submitted to the Board of Rites for final approval.

The chief duty of the City Guardian was to protect the city from evil. He represented Heaven and after Buddhism had established purgatory he also represented Yama of the lower world. His special function was to keep a vigilant eye on the acts of men and report the same to Heaven and deliver the sinner up to Yama. He was also the patron deity of the yamen runners.

The temples of this deity usually occupy the central part of the city and are very popular. The god is taken out in procession in the spring when he releases the spirits. On the first day of the seventh month he is taken out again to count the spirits. On the first day of the tenth month he is supposed to collect the spirits and shut them up for the winter.

The procession in the tenth month was the most elaborate. In the olden days of the Manchu dynasty, the images of the City Guardian and his sons, of whom he had several, were usually under the care of societies who looked after the idol and took it out in processions. The members of these societies belonged to the highest families and the positions in them were coveted by ambitious social climbers. The members collected money toward the coats of paint and garments and other paraphernalia needed by the gods and as a reward for their labours, they were given the privilege of carrying a basket of incense in the procession. After the procession they partook of a bountiful feast and enjoyed the theatricals given in honour of the god.

The procession itself was a magnificent affair surpassing in grandeur the display of barbaric princes in their triumphant entries into conquered cities. It was an epitome of the rich religious history of the Chinese. At the head of the procession

OFFERING FOR LONG LIFE.

were the men with large signs with the characters, "Be reverently quiet," "Stand aside." Then followed two long lines of men with boards with gilded characters expressing the grandiloquent titles granted to the god by imperial decrees. These were followed by drummers and by musicians blowing their shrill instruments. Then lictors with high black conical hats, relics of the Mongol dynasty, slouched along, some with whips, and others dragging heavy bamboos rattling over the rough pavement and bringing terror to evil doers. The large red umbrella with many folds, the symbol of high rank, and the official fan moved with dignity behind the lictors. Then two by two filed long lines of the elite of the city. The tall brother, an idol ten or more feet high, with wooden head and bamboo frame covered by flowing garments carried by a man inside, stalked along. Behind him trundled the black brother with his oily complexion and gleaming eyes. Both of these were deputies of the higher gods and were terrors to wicked spirits and evil men.

Then came baskets with burning incense, flowers and fruit carried by men at the ends of sticks placed across the shoulders. Idols bobbed up and down on horses; children decked out in the colours of the rainbow sat like statues upon Mongolian ponies.

Prominent in the procession was a large round brass mirror, a replica of the mirror in purgatory in which the sinner finds not only himself revealed, but also the punishment reserved for him. Above the mirror is the motto: "Before the mirror of retribution there is no just man."

At the end of the long pageant of colour and religious imagery was carried in a sedan the City Guardian with a crown of pearls and arrayed in a long robe embroidered with dragons.

The line of march extended through the whole city. Along the streets the shops and houses prepared a table with incense, flowers, candles, and three small cups with tea leaves. As the procession passed, the head of the house performed appropriate worship at this improvised altar.

In the city of Foochow the procession was spread over two days. The idol was taken out of the walled city and spent the night in the house of a wealthy family in the suburbs. This honour of entertaining the idol was much sought for although it involved great expense and inconvenience. Such a house was considered immune to the ravages of disease and death for the year. If anyone in the house was possessed by a demon he was usually cured of his malady by the presence of this god who is the terror of all evil spirits. On the following day the procession wound through the main streets of the suburbs and returned to the temple within the walled city. The feast which followed was most sumptuous and was a social affair of the greatest importance.

This celebration is a favourable time to make vows. If one of the parents is sick, or if the family has met with misfortune the eldest son dons red garments, the characteristic colour of prisoners, or puts a chain about his neck, or a cangue around his head and presents himself at the temple of the god. The journey to the temple is interrupted every three, or nine steps by genuflections upon the pavement. On the cangue, or garments will often appear the characters meaning, " Help my mother to live long," " I vow respectfully to collect papers with characters." This individual would spend many days gathering scraps of paper with characters on them and burn the same in a special furnace provided for the purpose. At the temple worship is duly performed by burning incense and kneeling.

These processions synchronized with the time of the year when cholera, plague, and other diseases began to afflict the inhabitants of the crowded cities. These afflictions were attributed to demons. Quite frequently after such a procession disease was more prevalent because the germs were spread, but in spite of this the customs were kept up because they stimulated community co-operation and produced a spirit of optimism indispensable in the trying situations of life.

CHAPTER XXXII

THE WINTER SOLSTICE

The winter solstice is one of the most important festivals. It is essentially the festival of the family circle. Every member of the family turns homeward if he can possibly do so. In olden times the prisoners were allowed to go home at this season, a custom which has been kept up almost to the present day in various places.

The characteristic feature of this festival at Foochow is the making by all the members of the family of small dumplings of rice flour. On the evening before the day of the winter solstice all the members of the family gather about a table in the kitchen, or in the room behind the main reception room before the ancestral tablets. On the table is a large bamboo tray with ten pairs of red chopsticks, ten large oranges and several mandarin oranges with the flowers of the seasons stuck in them. The Mowtan peony represents spring, the lotus flower summer, the aster autumn, and then flowering almond winter. In the midst of these flowers is a miniature image of a small boy. On either side of the tray are larger images of boys. A bouquet of garlic tied with a red band with the usual candles, vases with flowers and an incense burner complete the outfit. This offering mirrors the desires of the family group. The ten chopsticks utter the prayer that the family circle may be kept intact. The number ten, a complete number, reinforces the meaning of the sound for chopsticks " present ". The sound for orange also means " good luck ". The flowers symbolize the seasons.

The images of boys utter the agelong desire of the Chinese for male progeny. The garlic signifies by its sound " numerous progeny ".

When all is ready the head of the family performs the customary worship. Then a lump of dough made by the bride of the year from rice flour is brought in and the members of the family gather about the table and roll small dumplings from the dough. A joyful expectant quiet pervades the company. There is no joking or laughing for fear that something unpropitious might be uttered.

The next morning before daylight the dumplings are cooked and rolled in flour, brown sugar, and sesame seed and presented to the ancestors and household gods. Some of them are stuck above the doors and on the doorposts. The breakfast on this day consists of these dumplings. The wife sends a dish of them to her mother. In certain parts of China the people prepare small red beans. After eating the beans they pour the water on the ground and say that they are warding off pestilence. At noon, or in the evening there is a feast. In the evening the candles and incense are lighted before the ancestors and household gods.

The round dumplings according to popular tradition, represent perfection, completion, and express the prayer that the family group may be kept intact during the year and also that a spirit of harmony and mutual love may bind it together.

A custom which has the authority of hoary antiquity is still followed on this day in various parts of China. The young wife presents her father-in-law and her mother-in-law with shoes and stockings embroidered with a mandarin duck and drake. These express the hope that the wearers may live to walk many years.

Not only are the elders honoured, but the high officials repaired before daylight to the temple where the emperor's tablet was worshipped with the k'ou t'ou.

The Chinese have sought by various methods to determine the exact day of the winter solstice. Of course at present it is determined by the use of modern astronomical methods, but a few of the old ways may be of interest. On this day the stag was said to shed its horns, and the blue lily to send forth its shoots and the water in the stream to stir. A primitive method was to place earth in one side of the scales and charcoal on the other, making them balance. When the change of vapour at the solstice took place the charcoal was heavier than the earth. A common way was to measure the shadow cast by the gnomon and to note the place of the sun among the stars.

The ancient belief was that the sun changed the character of its fire at this time and so man to assist the sun also changed his fire. According to the Chou Li in the summer the trees on the south side of the mountain were burned and thus the *yang* or male principle was stimulated and in the winter a few trees were taken from the north side of the mountain and soaked in water and thus the *yin* or female principle was assisted in its work.

The day has always been regarded as favourable for the prognostication of the weather, the crops, the price of grain and numerous other things during the coming year. An east wind means calamity, a west wind indicates that grain will ripen, south wind presages expensive grain while a north

WANG T'IEN KUNG, A DEMON EXPELLER.

wind promises a bountiful year. If the clouds precede, or follow the sun the coming year will be prosperous, peaceful, and free from pestilence. If there are no clouds the harvest will be small and the year bad. If the clouds are red there will be drought, if they are black there will be floods, white clouds foretell war and yellow clouds mean a bountiful year.

This is the time when various things are to be avoided. In Szechuan no soup is taken lest it should bring wet weather when the one who has eaten it makes a journey during the following year. After dinner they feed the fruit trees by placing rice in the notch of the tree. An old book advises the reader to sleep on straw under the north wall of the house in order to receive the creative vapours which are supposed to come at this time.

This is above all a time to follow a prescribed regimen as to food and conduct of life in order to assist the harmonization of the *yin* and *yang* vapours. The positive principle, *yang*, is born at this time and the negative principle, *yin*, begins to decrease. The superior man secluded himself, and kept quiet. He abstained from music and sexual intercourse and from food which stimulates activity of any kind.

This was also the day of the offering to Heaven by the emperor at the altar of Heaven south of Peking.

CHAPTER XXXIII
THE EIGHT SPIRITS

This festival was the offering at the end of harvest to the Eight Ch'a, the spirits who assisted the husbandman in his work. It was inaugurated by Shen Nung (2737–2697 B.C.), the divine husbandman, who invented the plough and taught the people to cultivate the soil. These eight spirits were Shen Nung, Hou Chi who was the director of husbandry, the tutelary god of the cultivator, of the watch-towers, of the wild animals, of the deities of ponds and dykes, of the water courses, and of the insect tribe. Others were added in the course of time, until in the Sung dynasty they numbered one hundred and ninety-two, but the name remained unchanged.

In ancient times the festival was observed both by the officials and the people. A prayer dating from early days sums up the purpose of the occasion :—" May the earth be at peace, may the water return to the pool, may the insects do no injury and may the grass and trees grow luxuriantly." Like all offerings it had two purposes. One was to requite these deities for past services, but the more important object was to stimulate them to improve their work during the coming year.

The festival has been merged with the *lie* festival. Traces of it still survive in various parts of China, but it has been over-shadowed by other festivals.

CHAPTER XXXIV

THE HUNTERS' FESTIVAL

This festival had its origin in the hunting period of Chinese civilization. The old *lie* character is made up of two parts, one meaning dog and the other rat, and the entire symbol means to hunt. The modern form of the character is made up of the sign for flesh and the one for rat.

The hunting season was inaugurated by offering a white cock to the spirits of the hunt. The cock is the harbinger of sunrise and so was regarded as possessing the same power over demons as the sun.

As the hunter was left behind by advancing civilization the festival was observed on the day following the winter solstice for the purpose of driving away evil influences and spirits. Through the different dynasties elaborate processions were organized for the purpose of driving out diseases prevalent at this season.

At present the festival is not generally observed in China, though in some parts it still has a place among the religious feasts. The Buddhists have adopted it to commemorate the day when Sakyamuni left his home to become a Buddha. He commanded that people cook gruel and feed the hungry spirits. In parts of Chihli province the people place broth made of rice, beans, and fruits, with pieces of ice upon the fruit trees so as to stimulate the fruit to ripen in the coming year. In other districts of this province the silkworms are watered. The boys also have their heads shaved and the girls have their ears pierced. The broth is also eaten for the purpose of fortifying the body against all diseases.

Traces of this hunters' festival may be found in many parts of China, but new conditions have introduced different elements. Only the character points to the simple offering of the primitive Chinese hunter.

CHAPTER XXXV

CLEANSING PROCESSIONS

The cleansing processions are a very ancient institution in China. The common belief that disease is caused by demons is a corrollary of the classical philosophy of the Chinese. According to this philosophy all the phenomena of nature are produced by the interaction of two principles, the *yin* and the *yang*. *Yin* is the principle which belongs to cold, darkness, and death. It is the mother of spectres and demons which produce disease and death. *Yang* is the principle of warmth, light, and life. It is associated with the sun and has power to overcome the *yin* and hence can overcome all disease and even death itself. Man may employ the power of *yang* to overcome the power of the *yin*. These two principles clearly grasped will enable us to understand the processions of the common people. They will enable us to understand the position of the scholar who ridicules these crude efforts to expel demons. Both the common man and the scholar are standing upon the same ground. The scholar has a more refined philosophy of the *yin* and the *yang*, but the means he employs in order to drive out disease are just as magical as those accompanied by the sound of drum and gong. Whether he suggests the use of *yang* medicine, or the use of powerful classical formulæ he is resorting to magic to overcome *yin* by the *yang*.

From ancient days the times of these cleansing processions have been fixed in the second month of spring, the second month of autumn and soon after the winter solstice. These are the months when the *yin* principle is especially active. The vernal equinox falls in the second month of spring, the autumnal equinox comes in the second month of autumn. At these times the *yin* and *yang* are almost equal in power and there is a tremendous struggle for supremacy on the part of the *yin*. This produces disease and hence the processions to overcome the disease. These times have also corresponded to the season of plague and sickness in China. The cleansing processions, however, are not confined to these days. They take place whenever disease afflicts the people.

We shall understand these principles best from quotations from the classical sources. The Chou Li says: "The inspectors of the region, four wild-looking fellows in dark coats and red skirts covered with bear skins, with four eyes glittering like gold, brandishing their weapons and waving their shields, led a hundred underlings in a cleansing procession, searched the houses and drove out disease." The commentary on this passage says: "When the *yang* is in the ascendant it rages. When *yin* is hiding, it produces disease. The wild-looking fellows represent the principle *yang* in its overbearance. They lead out the vicious demons of the *yin* and conquer and suppress them."

The most complete explanation of the cleansing processions is found in the Li Chi. In the portion called Yüeh Ling we read: "In the last month of spring the country is ordered to perform a cleansing procession. At the nine gates the victims were cut into pieces and in this way the evil spirits were warded off. Thereby they helped to complete the vapours of spring." The commentary on this passage is interesting.

TAOIST SWALLOWING A SWORD.

"The Great Tomb consists of the eight stars north of the Musca Borealis. They regulate death and burial. Within the Pleiades is a great mound which has gathered the vapours of dead bodies. When these vapours escape, then ferocious devils follow them and come out. The first part of this month the sun is in the constellation Musca Borealis and goes from Musca Borealis to the Pleiades. Therefore the expulsion of disease takes place at this time."

The Yüeh Ling further says: "In the second month of autumn the son of Heaven performs a cleansing procession and thereby he enables the vapours of autumn to penetrate all beings." Further, the same authority says: "In the last month of the winter the proper officials are ordered to perform a great cleansing procession. They cut up animals and place them on the gates of the four directions; they take out the clay cow and in this way send off the cold vapours."

The commentary on this passage adds light from astrology. It goes on: "This month the sun passes Aquarius, Pegasus and two stars of Ursa Major controlling human life. North of Aquarius are the two stars controlling imperial favour. North of the stars controlling life are two stars controlling danger. North of the two stars controlling imperial favour are two stars controlling the centre. North of the two stars controlling danger are these four groups of stars. They are the chiefs of the rulers of demons. Again the four stars of the Tomb are south-east of Pegasus. The vapours of the Tomb and the four regulators are able to cause ferocious devils to come out, to produce calamity and disease and hence the people have a procession, cut up victims and so ward off disease."

The Li Chi in the portion called Chiao T'e Sheng throws light on the attitude of Confucius toward these cleansing processions. "When the villagers were expelling the ferocious demons, Confucius dressed in court garments stood upon the eastern steps and so quieted the spirits of his household." The older commentators interpret this to mean that Confucius did this to quiet and comfort the spirits of his own household. When these spirits heard the noise outside they were naturally frightened and so Confucius to quiet them stood upon the eastern steps. Later commentators dominated by a more refined view of nature have opposed this view.

The Shih Chi added further evidence to the classical character of the cleansing processions. "Cut up a dog and place the pieces on the four gates of the city and thereby oppose the plague of venomous demons."

The above passages give the underlying principles. In the Books of the Later Han (A.D. 25–220) we find a description of these cleansing processions as practised by the emperor and the people at the capital of the country. Similar descriptions may be found in the history of the T'ang and Sung and other dynasties.

"One day before the *lie* day (soon after the winter solstice) there was a great cleansing procession called driving out disease. For this ceremony there were selected at the Chung Huang gate one hundred and twenty boys between the ages of ten and twelve to act as parade boys. All wore red turbans and black cloaks. In their hands they held large hand drums. The inspectors of the region with four yellow metal eyes, dressed in bear skins, with dark upper garments and red skirts, armed with weapons, waved their shields. There were twelve beasts with hair and horns. They went out of the Chung Huang Gate. The beggars and underlings led them out and thereby drove out the evil demons.

"Within the forbidden city in the early morning the court officials gathered the privy counsellors, the prime minister, the court annalist, the court herald, the commander of the imperial guard and the assistants, all with red turbans. The imperial guards mounted on chariots rode before the imperial court. The commander at the Huang Gate ordered the parade boys to "prepare and drive out the disease". Thereupon at the Chung Huang Gate the company led off and the parade boys responded in chorus as follows: "The Chia-tso eats evil; Fu-wei eats tigers; Hsiung-po eats the devils produced by cold objects; T'eng-chien consumes misfortune; Lan-chu devours calamity; Po-chi eats dreams; Chien-liang, Tsu-men together consume those devils who have died of injury, and those devils who are desiring to enter into life; Wei-sui eats all apparitions; Ts'o-tuan eats the great evil; Ch'iung-chi, T'eng-ken together eat poison. We shall employ the twelve spirits to drive out evil; they will scorch your bodies red; they will break your trunk and joints, they will tear your flesh; they will tear out your lungs and bowels. If you do not go away quickly and if you return they will make meat of you."

"The inspectors of the region with the twelve beasts make their manipulations and shout with a loud voice everywhere in front and behind making three rounds of inspection. They take lighted torches and send off the evil out of the Tuan Gate. Outside this gate the imperial grooms mounted pass the torches out of the palace. Outside of the gate of the palace of the minister of war the horsemen of the five divisions of the army put the torches into the Lo river.

"The hundred officials in their yamens may make a cleansing procession with animals having wooden faces. When the people and scholars have set up mannikins of Yü Lei and the Wei-chiao, the assistants and the imperial guards break off sedge lances and peach rods and present them to the ministers of the first rank and second rank, the generals and the feudatory princes."

The commentary on this passage quotes several ancient works and throws so much light on the Chinese conception of demons that I shall quote it in full. A work called the Old Customs of the Han Dynasty says: "Chuan Hsü (2513 B.C. the fifth of the five legendary emperors) had three sons who died at birth and became disease demons. One lived in the Yangtse river. He was a disease-producing devil. One lived in the Joh river. This one became Wang-liang and Yü-kuei (the Wang-liang is a demon who takes the form of a small child of brown colour with red eyes and long ears and lives in the water. The Yü-kuei dwells in the water and spurts sand at people as they pass by and bites their shadow in the water and thus injures them). One of the sons dwells in human habitations in nooks and corners and causes children to take fright."

The commentary quotes further the Yüeh Ling Chang Chü as follows: "When the sun is in the northern constellations, it is feared that the *yin* which belongs to the north will repress the *yang*. Therefore the officials are ordered to perform

SENDING OFF THE DEMONS OF DISEASE.

great cleansing processions. By these they assist the *yang* to repress the *yin*."

The commentary quotes also an old poem which has a martial strain : " Ward off mountain goblins, cut the legs of the evil demons ; cut the heads of Wei-shê demons ; take the brains out of the demons who dwell in the grassy swamps ; catch and shut up the drought devils. In the clear and ice-cold water drown the Puo female devils (also causing drought). In the pools of the gods destroy the demon apparitions dwelling in wood and stone and the eight brothers roaming among men." These devils are known and feared in Foochow to-day.

The Grand Historiographer of Han Shun Ti, Chang Heng (A.D. 78–139) gives the scholar's view of these matters as follows : " I have seen in the capital great calamity which caused the people to die of disease. Whole families were destroyed. Everybody was frightened. The court was anxious and very sad. It was my duty to investigate the causes and discover a remedy to ward off the calamity and save the people. I did not know the cause of the trouble and day and night I was active about this matter. I heard that the most important business of the country is sacrifice. Among the sacrifices none is greater than the sacrifice to Heaven and the offering to the ancestors. At present rumours are current on the streets. The people say that the emperor An Ti (A.D. 107–26) while making a journey of inspection in the south died on the way. The wicked officials who accompanied him desired to summon the princes of all the feudalities and so did not announce the death. They sent the garments and the chariot back to the palace and deceitfully called the great officials to go before the gods and pray for the life of the emperor. I was stationed at a distance and did not know these details. Why should not the exalted spirit of the emperor being so deceived be angry? An individual is punished by the gods for small acts of remissness. How much more the desecration of the rite of worshipping Heaven and the ancestors? Confucius said: (When one was about to make an improper offering to T'ai Shan) 'Does not T'ai Shan know more about ceremony than Lin Fang?' (a pupil of Confucius deficient in the knowledge of ceremony). Heaven and Earth clearly investigate; they send down trouble and calamity. This is their law.

"Moreover, if there was any occasion, the proper officials just after the winter solstice ordered to open the spirit way to the imperial tombs. The emperor is very filial and did not presume to oppose this. They opened the tomb and transferred the body. The Yüeh Ling says that in the second month you must not stir the earth. You should be careful not to open the tombs and employ many people. By this precaution you make firm and seal the vapours of earth. If the vapours of earth ooze out, it is called opening the rooms of heaven and earth. All hibernating animals will die and the people will be afflicted with sickness and pestilence and will scatter abroad. The vapours of the dead spirits are not at rest and I fear that they have done harm these last two years. I wish you to know this and repent."

It is hardly necessary to describe the modern cleansing processions because they differ very little from those performed in the Han dynasty and in the days when Confucius viewed them from his steps. If a village, or a ward of a city is afflicted by an epidemic a committee collects money for an idol procession. They receive gifts from three cents up. They prepare torches, drums, large lanterns, gongs, and cymbals. From the neighbourhood temple they take the idols called the tall brother and the small brother. These two idols consist of head, bust, and long flowing robes. They are placed upon a pole and a man takes his place inside the long garments and stalks through the streets preceded by the torches, lanterns, drums, and gongs. They pass through the village several times making as much noise as possible.

In some of the processions small boys are carried on the shoulders of men, or on floats.

Some of these processions are called "driving the devils into the sea". Into a large boat consisting of a bamboo frame covered with paper with a dragon head and gleaming eyes are placed offerings also made of paper. The idea among the people is that the demons seeing such a beautiful and well supplied boat will enter into it. Before the boat starts a feast is given to the gods who drive out the devils and also to the devils. The procession worms its way through the crowded streets. The larger the crowd the better, for the devils fear crowds. The drums and gongs make a deafening noise. In the procession a man carries on a pole across his shoulder two buckets with pig's hair, goat's hair, and refuse from the animals slaughtered symbolizing the demons. The boat is burned or sent down stream. The buckets of dirt are dumped into the river and so the village is rid of the demons and their work. The people return to their occupations with a new hope that better days are ahead of them.

CHAPTER XXXVI

THE GOD OF THE HEARTH

Two objects of worship are found in all parts of China, the ancestral tablet and the god of the hearth or the kitchen god. Not only are these two practically universal, but they date from a remote antiquity and have passed through an interesting history.

The god of the hearth has a peculiar interest not merely because he is the most intimate deity of the Chinese family, surpassing the ancestors in the friendliness with which he is regarded, but he is interesting because he is a composite god having taken unto himself certain functions which in former days were performed by others. In fact he has displaced at least one god.

The history of this development discloses an interesting phase of religious evolution. The first component of this god is fire. Fire was regarded as something divine long before men thought of divinity in the likeness of man. By means of fire man was able to prepare for himself proper nourishment. Its curling snakelike flames shooting upwards ever fascinated him as he stood over it and warmed himself. It seemed to transform mundane objects into gifts to the gods and carry them away on its smoke up into the sky where the gods dwell, and so it was early regarded as the messenger of the gods who took man's offering to the beings on high.

Later, in the State and popular worship a god of fire was developed who presided over fire and its activities. The

KITCHEN GOD.

ancient Chinese called him Chu Yung which means "saluting the vapours". He is said to have been one of the six ministers of the emperor Huang Ti (2697–2596 B.C.) and to have ruled over the south. After his death he became one of the spirits of the universe and was placed over the element fire. He was early represented with a human face and with the body of an animal. This mythological episode illustrates the process of humanizing natural forces and also illustrates the separation of fire on earth and fire as represented in the summer sun which comes from the south and brings spring and summer to the northern world.

This deity was regarded as the tutelary god of the three months of summer and the people and officials made their offering to him in the first and last month of summer on the hearth. There were also temples to the god of fire in every walled city at which offerings were made in the summer. This offering has been discontinued under the republic, the temples are neglected and only visited after a great conflagration.

While the god of fire was connected with the southern sun and with the element fire, his most intimate history is to be found in the home. In order to appreciate this we shall have to visualize the early Chinese house. This was usually a cave dug in a bank, or consisted of a low hut constructed with timbers covered over with dirt and leaves. In the roof over the centre was an opening through which the smoke escaped. This is called in ancient books "the centre of the house", or "the place where the rain came in". The place under this opening was sacred to the tutelary god of the ground on which the house stood. It was watered by the rains and dews of heaven and watched over by the sun and moon. It was the place where the food of the family was prepared and eaten and the spot where family councils were held. It was here where the god was worshipped who combined in himself the mystery of the fire, the guardianship of the place upon which the house stood and the growing traditions and ideals of the family. The Chinese house has been enlarged and improved, but the house is still built about a court " where the rain comes in ". The kitchen has been moved and with it the god of the hearth, but the goddess of the eaves still continues the tradition of the god of the centre of the house.

The god of fire, the guardian deity of the house and the guardian of the family added one more deity before they coalesced into the present god of the hearth. The ancient Chinese had a tutelary god of life who presided over such matters as length of life, misfortune, reward, and punishment. This deity was at first among those worshipped by the emperor and his officials, but was early taken up by the common people. This god was early identified with the upper two stars of the foot of Ursa Major and was worshipped in the last month of the year by burning a pyre. The god of the hearth became the earthly representative of this stellar god. Still later the stellar god was subordinated to Heaven or the God of Heaven and the kitchen god became the representative of the God of Heaven on earth. The great offering was transferred to the end of the year at which time the kitchen god went up to Heaven to report upon the sins and good deeds of the family.

Just when this process implicit in the situation from the beginning culminated it is difficult to say. The Chinese ascribe it to the emperor Wu Ti (140–85 B.C.) who paid special worship to the kitchen god with a view to gaining power with Heaven and becoming an immortal through his good reports. However that may be, we find the god of the kitchen the centre of the family religion. He is regarded as the deputy of Heaven to watch over the affairs of the family and to report at the end of the year at the Court of Heaven on the same. He thus combined the interests circling about the hearth, the idea of fire as the messenger of the gods and also the idea as the deputy of the gods to watch over the affairs of the family and to report to Heaven.

The custom of sending off the god of the hearth at the end of the year to report to Heaven was well established during the Sung dynasty (A.D. 960–1278) and has continued on to the present day. On the twenty-third day of the twelfth month the meat offering is made and on the next day the vegetable offering. The families who offer one do not offer the other.

As the day closes and the twilight comes on, a table is spread in the kitchen before the stove, above which is pasted the picture of the god of the hearth and his spouse. In addition to the usual incense burner, candles, vases, food, and wine there are several plates of sweets and cakes of various shapes and colours. When all is ready the head of the house offers incense and kneels and bows while the members of the family stand. When this is completed he takes off the picture of the god and burns it in the urn near the table with a lot of idol paper money. As the flames shoot upward the members of the family repeat the words :—

"Come, god of the kitchen
Oh, grandfather Chang
Come, here is your pudding
And here is your t'ang (sugar)

    Go flit up to heaven;
    Begone in a trice;
    Forget all the bad
    And tell only what's nice."

The vegetable offering is similar to the meat offering. In certain households the place above the door of the stove is smeared with dregs of wine, or sugared dumplings are stuck about it. After the offering in some parts of China people throw beans over the roof of the house intended for the steed of the god. This festival is enjoyed by the children, for the god of the kitchen shares his candies with them.

The god of the hearth occupies a very important position in the social and religious life of the Chinese. Ko Hung, a writer of the fourth century, says:—"The spirit of high Heaven presiding over life investigates the evil and sin of men. From those who commit great sins the tutelary spirit of life takes away one year. From those who commit small sins he takes away one hundred days. In proportion to the lightness, or seriousness of the sins he takes away little or much." The god of the kitchen is the moral policeman who represents the God of Heaven in the home.

The kitchen is kept clean, that is, as clean as the circumstances and habits of the people permit. No ill smelling stuff, or bad wood is burned in the stove. Moreover, the women rarely scold in the kitchen nor are wicked plots hatched there. Before a member of the household starts out on a journey he burns incense before the kitchen god. The new bride worships the kitchen god after she has worshipped Heaven and Earth, and the ancestors.

When the family moves, after all the household goods have been taken away, the kitchen god is transferred to the new abode. A relative lights a bamboo torch in the old stove and precedes, or follows the moving family and then kindles the fire in the new hearth. Where the stove is a movable one it is carried through the streets with a fire of charcoal and thus the god of the hearth is transferred from one house to another.

A common way of obtaining light on future happenings is to inform the god of the kitchen about the undertaking and then to listen to conversations of passers-by on the street. The first sentence which is clearly apprehended is meditated on and conclusions as to the success of the undertaking deducted from it. Another method is to put a wooden ladle in the rice boiler and then going in the direction in which the handle points to pick up scraps of conversation from which guidance may be extracted. Often the individual puts his chopsticks into his sleeve before he has finished the meal, and listens to the talk of people for the purpose of catching a guiding phrase.

We have followed the god of the hearth through the vicissitudes of his varied history. To-day he is still the centre of the Chinese family life of almost equal importance with the ancestors. This position he occupies because he is the connecting link between the family and its members and the Great Heaven who loves and rules all men.

CHAPTER XXXVII

THE SACRIFICE TO HEAVEN DURING THE MANCHU DYNASTY

Outside of the Tartar city of Peking in the Chinese city is situated a large park in which stands the altar of Heaven. The enclosure has an area of over a square mile and consists of an outer court and an inner court shaded by old cypress trees. The whole is surrounded by a wall which is curved at the north end in the same manner as the walls around graves.

The round mound or the altar of Heaven is built of white marble and consists of three concentric terraces approached by stairs of nine steps to each terrace from the four points of the compass. The top terrace is 90 feet in diameter, the second terrace is 150 feet, and the lower terrace is 210 feet. The top terrace has a circular stone in the centre. In the first circle are nine stones, then eighteen. There are nine such circles. The outermost circle contains eighty-one stones. The terraces and stairs are flanked by carved balustrades. In the sides of the terraces there are 360 panels. These measurements are multiples of the odd numbers from one to nine, which symbolize Heaven.

The circular court about the altar, 335 feet in diameter, is surrounded by a low wall covered with blue tiles. At each cardinal point of the compass there is an opening with three doors. The circular court is surrounded by a square court 549 feet on each side. In the south-west corner of this court stood three masts with lanterns. The south-east corner is

THE ALTAR OF HEAVEN, PEKING.

occupied by a large furnace of green tiles in which the bullock was burned. Near by are eight iron braziers for burning the offerings of silk.

North of the altar a small round building with a conical roof of blue tiles contains the tablets and tabernacles of Shangti and the ancestors. On one side among the trees stands a group of buildings employed to store the sacrificial implements. On the other side is the hall of abstinence in which the emperor kept vigil before the great sacrifice. Outside of the south gate of the square court on the east side was the place of the dressing tent of the emperor. It was provided with a fireplace for the purpose of warming the tent.

On the north side of the altar is a covered circular building on a foundation of three circular terraces. This is often wrongly called the temple of Heaven. It was the temple in which the emperor prayed for a good year.

All the rites and ceremonies of State of the last dynasty were in charge of the Board of Rites. It had two presidents, one Manchu and one Chinese, and four vice-presidents, two Manchus and two Chinese, and numerous petty officials. The sacrifice to Heaven was in charge of the Court of Supreme Imperial Sacrifices. This court had two presidents, one Manchu and one Chinese, and two vice-presidents, one Manchu and one Chinese, and a large number of under-officials and secretaries. It looked after all the sacrifices offered by the emperor, or his proxies.

In sacrifices of the first class the one who officiated and his assistants purified themselves for three days. For a sacrifice of the second class they purified themselves for two days. Accordingly three days before the sacrifice early in the morning the Court of Sacrificial Worship, being a department of the Court of Supreme Imperial Sacrifices, brought the abstinence tablet to the emperor. This tablet was two inches long and one inch wide covered with yellow paper. It had inscribed upon it in Chinese and Manchu the day of abstinence. It was worn on the breast. The Emperor issued a proclamation to all his officials regarding the practice of abstinence as follows: "In a certain year, month, day, at the winter solstice, I shall sacrifice to Shangti of August Heaven at the round mound. Now all officials purify your heart, cleanse your desires. Let all exalt their duty. Should anyone be disrespectful the dynasty has a fixed punishment. Be respectful. Do not be remiss." This proclamation was posted in the main hall of the yamens. All officials of the seventh rank and above practised abstinence in their official residences.

Those who practised abstinence did not occupy themselves with public affairs, nor with criminal cases. They did not attend banquets and abstained from music, sexual intercourse, wine, and vegetables with a strong odour such as onions. They did not visit the sick, nor did they go to the tombs of their ancestors, nor did they assist in the sacrifice to the dead or the gods. On the evening before the sacrifice they took a bath.

Five days before the sacrifice a prince of the blood examined the sacrificial victims and pronounced them perfect. Two days before the sacrifice the animals were inspected again by the president of the Board of Rites.

Two days before the great ceremony the prayer offered to Heaven at the sacrifice was written on a tablet. Before dawn the reader of the sacrificial prayer brought a tablet on which the prayer was to be written to the emperor's Privy Council and handed it to the imperial secretaries. These officials placed the tablet in a purified room and wrote the prayer on it. The prayer was then deposited on a yellow table in the executive mansion. The grand secretary came to the table, examined the prayer and affixed the imperial name. The next day the prayer tablet was given to the one who read the prayer.

One day before the sacrifice from 11 p.m. to 1 a.m. the animals were killed and the blood was buried. On the same day the altar of Heaven was swept and the places were arranged for the tablet of Shangti on the north side of the highest terrace facing the south. The places for the tablets of T'ai Tsu (1616–26), Shih Tsu (1644–61), Shih Tsung (1723–35), Jen Tsung (1796–1820), Wen Tsung (1851–61), were arranged on the east side of the terrace and the places for the tablets of T'ai Tsung (1627–43), Sheng Tsu (1662–1722), Kao Tsung (1736–95), Hsüan Tsung (1821–50), Mu Tsung (1862–74), on the west side.

On the second terrace places were arranged for the tablets of the sun, moon, the seven stars of the dipper, the five planets, the twenty-eight constellations, the signs of the zodiac, the god of the clouds, the god of rain, the god of wind, and the god of thunder. The various receptacles for the offerings were put before the places of the tablets at the same time.

The time for the imperial cavalcade to go to the altar was fixed by the Imperial Board of Astronomy. It took place the day before the great sacrifice. The people were duly warned to keep off the road by which the procession passed.

This procession was a magnificent affair, an epitome of the mythology and religious history of the Chinese people. The centre figure was the emperor. There were guards, musicians, marshals, flags with embroidered dragons, with the sun and moon, clouds, thunder, wind, rain, the banners of the twenty-eight constellations borne by twenty-eight men; there were the flags of the five planets, the flags of the five guardian mountains, the four rivers, the various constellations; there were flags for various birds; there were feathers and plumes, a revelry of colour and beauty. There were large red umbrellas with many folds.

After arrival the emperor examined the altar and the offerings and then retired into the palace of abstinence where he passed the night preparing himself for the great offering

During the night the president of the Bureau of Sacrificial Offerings with his assistants lit the golden lamp and the candles piled up the wood and put the ox on it and placed the offerings on the dishes before all the tablets. On the top terrace they placed a table with the prayer-tablet. On another table they put a blue piece of jade and twelve rolls of silk.

The emperor at the sacrifice occupied the south end of the second terrace. The top terrace was occupied by the one who read the prayer, those who offered incense, the silk rolls, cups, the bearers of the cushions on which the emperor knelt, and the censors who observed the ceremony. On the lowest terrace above the steps were the princes from the first to the third order. Below the steps were the princes of the fourth order. Below this terrace were the musical instruments with 180 musicians and 300 posturers and a host of minor officials to the fifth civil rank and the fourth military rank.

On the day of the sacrifice seven quarters before sunrise the prayer-tablet was placed on the altar. The president of the Board of Rites lead the presidents of the Board of Sacrificial Worship to the tablets in order to invite the spirits to come into the tablets and partake of the offerings. The marshal of the Equipage Department placed the tablets into the niches prepared for them.

When this was done the emperor was led to his place on the altar and all the officials took their places.

The ceremony began by the emperor washing his hands. The pyre with the victim on it was kindled and the instruments struck up a hymn to invite the gods and spirits to partake of the sacrifice. The song is called the "Beginning of Harmony" and is as follows:—

"Respectfully we receive the blessings of Heaven.
 Oh! How they shine with magnificence!
 Now the country has been at peace for a long time.
 The people within the four seas are united.
 We offer a grand sincere sacrifice.
 In obedience to the laws of the twelve tubes we harmonize
   the winds.
 The unsearchable law of Heaven will grant a glorious blessing
 And Heaven will regard my mean self with affection.
  Profoundly I consider the exalted generosity
 And hope to be assisted in bringing to completion the works
   of Heaven.
 We have arranged in order the sacrifices.
 Day and night we make our wishes known to Heaven.
 Our chariots like clouds wait a long time,
 Horses and chariots fill the open space in great numbers.

Blue banners in great array flap in the wind.
They stand arrayed in numberless rows.
Reverently we begin to harmonize our feelings of joy
And look respectfully toward the azure vault.
Ye hundred spirits condescend to grant your protection
To the rulers who purify themselves.
Ye Shen come down to the banquet and enjoy yourselves.
Shangti is perspicacious.
Together they shine forth with mercy and favour
And regard from afar my virtue."

While the posturers were acting and the music sounding, the stewards in charge of the incense went before the tablets of Shangti and the ancestors and waited. The official in charge of the standard which gave the signals for the different parts of the ceremony raised the standard as a signal for the emperor to ascend the top terrace. The ushers led the emperor to the top terrace and remained standing at the table with the prayer-tablet. Other ushers led him to the tablet of Shangti. Those in charge of the incense were kneeling before the tablet of Shangti. At a call from the usher the emperor knelt. Incense was given to him and he lifted it up thrice. Then he arose and performed a similar ceremony before the tablets of the ancestors. Another signal was given and the emperor returned to his place on the second terrace where he remained standing. Then the emperor at a given signal knelt three times and at each kneeling bowed thrice. All the princes then performed the k'ou-t'ou. The music stopped and the master of ceremonies announced the offering of the jade and the silk. The music struck up the tune called the "Illustrious Peace".

"The dragon, unicorn, the tortoise and phœnix flags have arrived.
The instruments all tuned await the players.
The stewards with respect bring forward the platter with jade.
They manifest their sincere respect by swiftly
running forward with presents of beautiful gems and
quantities of silk in order arranged.
Come ye spirits in large numbers and receive our gifts.
With thoughts respectful
With great sincerity in perfect order
We make respectful announcement."

While the music was playing the emperor was led before the tablets of Shangti and the ancestors and offered the jade and the silk.

This ceremony finished, the tables with the victims were offered. The urn with the broth was taken before the tablets of Shangti and the ancestors and a small quantity of the broth was poured out three times. The music then struck up the tune called "Completed Peace", as follows :—

"We make an offering of fine boiled rice.
Respectfully we arrange vases of wood and bamboo.
We present the abundant offering arranged on the table
And deign to offer a pure and reverent offering.
Pork and goat, silk and chestnuts,
We present the fat and the raw meat.
We make our offering in clean gourds and calabashes
resembling Heaven's orb.
All is sweet like a water spring.
We desire that you should deign to descend and regard us.
Arrest thy cloudy chariot
And grant a bountiful blessing
During myriads of ten thousand years."

The emperor was led, while the music was playing, before the tablets and with a ceremony already described above offered the table with the meats.

The music struck up as follows :—

"The jade libation cups in order arranged
Emit a brilliant light.
The cinnamon scented wine begins to ferment,
Giving forth a fine odour.
So my heart receiving your mercy
Presents a cup full of sweet wine.
The sweet wine well mixed contains a blessing,
Its perfume like incense spreads afar.
May the gods' mercy protect and regard me with favour great and vast.
With hesitation and devoutness we gaze upward and wait.
Then restlessly we pace back and forth."

During the playing of the music the emperor was led to the tablets and offered the wine-cup.

The signal was then given to go to the prayer-table and the emperor was led before the table. The reader of the prayer also went before the prayer-table and performed the k'ou-t'ou. He then took the tablet with the prayer and knelt at the left of the table. The music ceased, the emperor knelt and all the officials knelt and in the quiet of the morning hour the prayer was read. The words were as follows : " In the present year, month, day, continuing in the line of the son of Heaven, I, N.N., presume to announce by decree to Shangti of August Heaven as follows : " At the winter solstice the six vapours begin their beneficial work (the six vapours are the *yin*, *yang*, the wind, the rain, darkness, and light), reverently honouring the rules of ceremony I conduct respectfully all the officers and bring jade, silk, sacrificial victims, grain, and vases of all kinds. This pure burnt offering I make respectfully to Shangti, to T'ai Tsu (1616–26), Kao Emperor, who inherited Heaven's universal rule. By thy holy virtue and divine power thou didst establish the fundamental principles of the empire. Thou wast benevolent, filial, of a penetrative mind, possessing military prowess, correct, firm, reverent, and peaceful; thy great perfection established the dynasty. (I address) my prayer to T'ai Tsung (1627–43), Wen Emperor, who conformed to Heaven's will and made the dynasty flourish. Vast thy virtue, brilliant thy military prowess; indulgent and mild, merciful and holy, of profound wisdom, filial, respectful, and intelligent. Brilliantly didst thou fix the exalted Tao, of illustrious merit. I address Shih Tsu (1644–61), Chang Emperor, who embodied Heaven's high decree. Thou didst establish the succession to the empire and lay down the fundamental principles; a penetrative mind, reverent and accomplished, illustrious in military powers, and of great virtue. Great thy merit and thy love. Thy filial piety was perfect. (I address) Sheng Tsu (1662–1722 K'ang Hsi), Jen Emperor, who harmonized Heaven's universal decree; of great literary ability and military power, profound in thought and prudent; reverent, temperate, indulgent, magnanimous; filial, respectful, true, sincere, moderate, peaceful, of great merit and virtue, the great perfect emperor, (I address) Shih Tsung (1723–35 Yung Cheng), Hsien Emperor. who respected Heaven's glorious decree; moderate anp correct; of literary ability and military prowess; brilliant and glorious, indulgent, loving, sincere, and firm; profound in wisdom, holy and of great filial piety. (I address) Kao Tsung (1736–95 Ch'ien Lung), Shun Emperor, who took as his model Heaven's sublime decree; holy and foreknowing, embodying Heaven's primordial power and establishing the fundamental rules of the empire; famous for his literary talent and an ardent warrior; reverent, intelligent, filial, merciful, divine, and holy. (I address) Jen Tsung (1796–1820 Chia Ching), Jui Emperor. Thou didst receive the will of Heaven to make the empire flourish. Thou didst spread civilization and wast peaceful in thy plans, eminent in culture, resourceful in war; filial, respectful, diligent, and moderate, correct, intelligent, brilliant, and prudent. May the associates honour our sacrifice."

When the reading of the prayer ended, the reader arose and placed the prayer-tablet in a basket before the tablet of Shangti. Then he performed the k'ou-t'ou and retired. While the music played the emperor and all the officials performed the k'ou-t'ou.

The emperor was then led to the tablet of the ancestors. The assistants were led to the tablets of the gods on the second terrace. They presented incense, silk, and cups of wine. This done, the emperor and the assistants were conducted back to their places. The music stopped. The military posturers retired and the civil posturers with plumes and flutes came forward.

The herald then announced the second offering. Those in charge of the cups came forward and the chief musician announced the second offering. The music struck up the tune called " Beautiful Peace ", as follows :—

"Strike the bells, start the evolutions,
  Bring forward again the gem wine-cup
  With profound respect we show our service.
  In order we respectfully bring our offering
  With the face pure and the countenance at ease,
  To the azure table of Heaven resplendent and glorious.
  Silently and joyfully Heaven partakes of the perfume of the offering,
  While the harmonious vapours well up like the ocean.
  All the people await the blessing.
  With respect they gaze up to the pearly vault of Heaven.
  The glorious fountain and the blessed dew
  Will bring reward without merit."

While the music was playing the posturers with plumes and flutes went through their evolutions. The emperor was conducted to the top terrace and offered the wine cup. After he returned to his place the last offering was announced. The music struck up the piece called the "Eternal Peace", as follows:—

"Oh! the final offering!
  Pure is the jade cup.
  Respectfully we offer the millet wine.
  We bring the seasoned broth.
  The jade stones and the flute sound *tsiang tsiang*.
  The sacrifice is absolutely perfect.
  The good wine overflows.
  Do not cease until your purpose is complete.
  The clear will of Heaven should be looked up to and examined.
  Then Heaven will bless the multitude of living beings.
  The eight dragons move forward.
  All the instruments of music play in harmony."

Evolutions like those of the previous offering were performed by the posturers. The emperor was conducted to the top terrace and offered the wine cup on the right side with the same ceremony as before. He was conducted to his place where he remained standing. At each offering the assistants made similar offerings to the tablets on the second terrace.

When the final offering was ended an usher went before the table of the prayer-tablet and announced the receiving of the viand of blessing. The president of the Court of Imperial Entertainment received the viand of blessing and placed it on the table before Shangti. The announcement was then made to go to the place of drinking the blessing and receiving the viand.

The emperor was conducted before the altar of Shangti and drank the wine of blessing and received the viand of blessing from the two directors of the Court of Imperial Entertainment. After this the emperor and all the officials performed the k'ou-t'ou.

The herald then announced the removing of the offerings. The music struck up the piece called the "Flourishing Peace", as follows:—

" The whole *yang* returns again.
The united vapours increase in power.
The bowls for washing the hands are brought forward
And arranged clean and white.
The offering is then removed.
We dare not presume to be slow in taking it away.
The ceremony is about to come to an end.
The music sounds notes of great joy.
We look upward toward the nine heavens

As the Lord of day returns great and glorious
And sends down blessing,
And assists the people."

While the music was playing those in charge of the jade and silk went before the tablet of Shangti and offered the azure jade.

The master of ceremonies then announced the escorting off of the spirits who had come to the sacrifice. The music struck up the piece called "Pure Peace", as follows :—

"Oh! ascend to the altar and announce the sacrifice accomplished.
The altar and terrace are hidden by clouds of incense odours.
With reverence we look back and behold
The chariots of the Shen like clouds going in great numbers.
I pray for the blessings of the seasons.
May you be moved and consider our offering of sweet incense.
Relying upon thy favour we ardently desire that you may produce
Many scholars who will assist the dynasty.
May Heaven send rain and dew and the earth nourish all beings.
May the hundred grains be luxuriant and flourishing.
Multiply our excellent advisors
Who will advise a straight and correct way and promote peace and quiet."

While the music was playing the emperor and all the officials performed the k'ou-t'ou. When they arose the instruments ceased.

The master of ceremonies then announced that the prayer-tablet, the silk, and the viands should be taken to the furnace. The emperor faced the west awaiting the articles to pass by him.

The master of ceremonies then announced to all to face the furnace and the instruments struck up the "Supreme Peace" tune as follows :—

" The grand ceremony is ended
  Revealing the sincere feelings of the heart.
  With respect the torch is applied to the offering
  And it burns with a surpassing odour.
  The thunder mounts its chariot, the lightning starts on its way.
  The nine dragons rise up,
  The purple vapours fill the four directions.
  The banners flap in the wind,
  All the people receive a blessing
  Complying with the five constant virtues.
  I, small child, respect the commands
  And hope to be blessed forever."

While the music was playing the emperor and his assistants at the sacrifice were led opposite the furnace to see the offerings burned up. The herald then announced the ceremony completed.

The music struck up the " Protecting Peace " as follows :—

" For Heaven's great blessing I bring solemn offerings.
  The flames of the sacrifice ascend and make announcement to Heaven.
  Only the Holy One is able to receive the sacrifice.

The gods of Heaven sit in the car drawn by six dragons,
They mount on the purple vapours.
May I long keep the decree of Heaven and extend the rule
of the empire."

The sacrifice is completed. The emperor and the great retinue return. The altar of Heaven is cleared. The abstinence tablets are removed. The stillness of the azure heaven again broods over the altar as it did at the dawn of Chinese civilization.

LIST OF WORKS CONSULTED

A. EUROPEAN

EDOUARD CHAVANNES. *Mémoires historiques de Se-ma Ts'ien traduits et annotés par Edouard Chavannes.*
EDOUARD CHAVANNES. *T'ai Chan.*
S. COUVREUR, S.J. *Li Ki.*
P. HENRI DORÉ, S.J. *Recherches sur les Superstitions en Chine.*
JUSTUS DOOLITTLE. *Social Life of the Chinese.* 1865.
ERNEST J. EITEL. *Handbook of Chinese Buddhism.*
R. C. FORSYTH. *Shantung the Sacred Province of China.* 1912.
HERBERT A. GILES. *A Chinese Biographical Dictionary.*
HERBERT A. GILES. *Strange Stories from a Chinese Studio.*
J. J. M. DE GROOT. *Les Fetes Annuellement Célébrées à Émoui.* 1886.
J. J. M. DE GROOT. *The Religious System of China.*
WILHELM GRUBE. *Zur Pekinger Volkskunde.*
WILHELM GRUBE. *Geschichte der Chinesischen Litteratur.* 1902.
L. HODOUS. *Buddhism and Buddhists in China.*
REGINALD FLEMING JOHNSTON. *Lion and Dragon in Northern China.*
WILLIAM FREDERICK MAYERS. *The Chinese Reader's Manual.*
JOHN STEELE. *I Li or Book of Etiquette and Ceremonial.* Probsthain.
R. P. M. TCHANG, S.J. *Synchronismes Chinois.*
A. WYLIE. *Notes on Chinese Literature.*

B. CHINESE

Analects of Confucius, Discourses of Confucius 論語

Book of Changes, Yih Ching 易經

Chia Yü 家語
Chiao T'e Sheng 郊特牲
Chou Li 周礼

Chuang Tzu 莊子
Chung Chien Yü Li Chih Pao Ch'ao 重鐫玉歷至寶鈔
Chung Yung, Doctrine of the Mean 中庸
Chu Shu Chi Nien 竹書紀年
Ch'an Men Erh Sung 禪門日誦
Ch'in Ting Szu K'u Ch'üan Shu Chien Ming Mu Lu 欽定四庫全書簡明目錄
Ch'in Ting Szu K'u Ch'üan Shu Tsung Mu 欽定四庫全書總目
Ch'in Ting Ta Ts'ing Huei Tien 欽定大清會典
Ch'in Ts'u Sui Shih Chi 荊楚歲時記
Ch'un Ch'iu 春秋

Dissipation of Sorrow, fourth century B.C. 離騷

Erh Chih Lu 日知錄

Feng Su T'ung 風俗通
Fu Chien T'ung Chih 福建通志

Hai Nei Shih Chou Chi 海內十洲記
Han Wei T'sung Shu 漢魏叢書
Hou Han Shu 後漢書
Hsi Ching Tsa Chi 西京雜記
Hsi Yü Chi 西域記 by a Buddhist monk Yuan Chuang, who recorded the experience of his journey through Central Asia and India completed in A.D. 646.
Hsi Yu Chi 西遊記
Hsia Hsiao Cheng 夏小正
Hsiao Ching 孝經
Hsieh P'en Huei Shang Pao Ching 血盆會上寶經
Huai-nan Tzŭ, d. 122 B.C. 淮南子
Huang Li, Calendar 皇歷

Jen Ming Hsü Chih 人名須知
Jung Chün Ming Sheng Chi Yao 榕郡名勝輯要

Kao Shang Yü Huang Pen Hsing Chi Ching 高上玉皇本行集經
Kuan Sheng Ti Chün Sheng Chi T'u Chi 關聖帝君聖蹟圖記
Kuan Ti Ming Sheng Chen Ching 關帝明聖眞經
Kuan Tzü 管子, his complete name was 管夷吾, minister of Ts'i in the seventh century B.C. The book is by later writers.
Kuan Yin Ts'i Tu Pen Yüan Chen Ching 觀音濟度本願眞經
Kung Kuo Kê 功過格
Ku Shan Chih 鼓山志

Land and Water Classic 山海經
Li Chi 礼記
Lieh Hsien Chuan 列仙傳
Liu Chai Chih I 聊齋志異
Lü Chen Jen Wen Chi 呂眞人文集
Lu Shih 路史
Lun Yü, Analects of Confucius 論語
Lung Ch'eng Lu 龍城錄, a spurious production of Wang Chih of the twelfth century.

Materia Medica 本草綱目 (1573-1620).
Mencius 孟子
Meng Hua Lu 夢華錄
Min Tu Chi 閩都記
Ming Tsa Chi 閩雜記
Monthly Rescripts of Li Chi 月令

Nan Hua Chen Ching 南華眞經

Old Customs of the Han Dynasty 漢舊儀
Old work of the sixth century, p. 190, 續齊諧記, compiled during Liang dyn. A.D. 502-57.

Pai Wen Ts'ung Lin Ch'ing Kuei Cheng I Chi 百文叢林清規證義記

Pai Hu T'ung 白虎通
Pen Ts'ao Kang Mu 本草綱目
Po Wu Chih 博物志

San Kuo Chih 三國志
San Kuo Chi Yen I 三國志演義
Shan Hai Ching 山海經
Shan Hai Ching T'u Shuo 山海經圖說
Shang Yu Lu 尚友錄
Shen Hsien Chuan 神仙傳
Shen I Ching 神異經
Shih Chi 史記
Shih Ching 詩經 Book of Poetry.
Shih I Chi 拾遺記 by 王嘉, *cir.* fourth century A.D.
Shu Ching 書經 Book of History.
Shui Ching 水經
Shuo Wen 說文
Small Regulator of the Hsia Dynasty 夏小正
So Shen Chi 搜神記
Ssu Ming Ti Chün Ching Tsao Ch'üan Shu 司命帝君敬竈全書
Sui Shih Chi 歲時記

Ta Hsüeh 大學 Great Learning
Tao Tê Ching 道德經
Tso Chuan 左傳
Tsun Sheng Pa Chien 遵生八牋, pub. 1591.
Tung Shan Lu 東山錄
Tung Yüeh T'ien Tsi Jen Sheng Ta Ti Pao Hsün 東嶽天齊仁聖大帝寶訓
T'ai P'ing Kuang Chi 太平廣記
T'ai Shang Kan Ying P'ien 太上感應篇
T'ai Shang San Kuan Ching 太上三官經
T'ao Yuan Min Sheng Ching 桃園明聖經
T'ien Hou Sheng Mu Sheng Chi Tsu Chih Ch'üan Chi 天后聖母聖蹟圖誌全集

Ts'u Tz'u 楚 辭
T'u Shu Chi Ch'eng 圖 書 集 成
T'ung Chien Kang Mu 通 鑑 綱 目

Wen Ch'ang Ti Chün Yin Ma Wen 文 昌 帝 君 陰 騭 文
Wen Ti Hsiao Ching 文 帝 孝 經

Yen Ching Sui Shih Chi 燕 京 歲 時 記. A calendar giving the customs of Peking.
Yih Ching 易 經 Book of Changes.
Yin Kuo Ching 因 果 經
Yu Yang Tsa Tsu 酉 陽 雜 俎 belongs to eighth century.
Yüeh Ling 月 令
Yü Li Ch'ao Chuan Ching Shih 玉 歷 鈔 傳 警 世
Yü Lan P'en Ching 盂 蘭 盆 經

LIST OF CHINESE NAMES

Amitabha (Omi-t'o-fo) 阿彌陀佛, 70

An Ti 安帝, 211

Bodhisattva 菩薩, 34, 73

Buddha 佛, 167, 203

Chang 張, 27

Chang Heng 張衡, 183, 186

Chang T'ien Shih 張天師, 127

Chia-tso 甲作, 209

Chia tzu 甲子, 23

Chieh Chih T'ui 介之推, 88

Chieh Chou 解州, 165, 170 f.

Ch'iang-liang 強梁, 209

Chih-yüan 紙鳶, 192

Ching Yen 敬炎, 86

Chu Yung 祝融, 215

Chuan Hsü 顓頊, 210

Chung Huang 中黃, 208, 209

Ch'eng Huang 城皇, 193

Ch'ien 乾, 26

Ch'ih Yu 蚩尤, 170

Ch'ing Ming 清朋, 86, 89, 91 ff.

Ch'ing Te, pure virtue 清德, 28, 31

Ch'iung-chi 窮奇, 209

Ch'ü Yüan 屈原, 136 f., 183

Ci-ci-chai, a colloquial phrase for shepherd's purse used in Foochow, v. He-ci-chai

Dang Dong 擔當, 5, 6

Eight Ch'a 八蜡, 202

Fu-wei 腹胃, 209

Hai 亥, 23, 75, 95

Han Hsin 韓信, 191

Han Shih 寒食, 86, 90 f.

He-ci-chai, Foochow colloquial for I chih ts'ai 壹恣荣, 100

Heng Shan, in Hunan 衡山, 113

Heng Shan 桓山, 113

Hou chiu chieh 後九節, 66

Hou T'u 后土, 146

Hou T'u Ch'i 后土祇, 146

Hsiung-po 雄伯, 209

Hua Shan, in Shensi 華山, 113

Huang 黃, 26

I chih 壹恣, 108

K'an diagram 坎 ☵, 187

Ko hung 葛洪, also 抱朴子, 218

Kou Mang, genius of spring 勾芒, 20, 24

Kuan P'ing 關平, 168

Kuan-Ti 關帝, 48, 62, 169 ff., 170 f.

Kuan Tzu 管子, 88

Kuang Yen Miao Yüeh 光炎妙月, 28

Kuanyin 觀音, 4, 50, 62, 68 f., 70, 73 f., 105, 109

Kuan Yü 關羽, 164 ff., 171
K'ai Min Wang 開閩王, 22
K'ou-t'ou 叩頭, 61 f., 226, 230, 232 f.
K'uei Hsing 魁星, 77 ff., 80 f.

Lan-chu 攬諸, 209
Li 離, 157
Lieh 獵, 202 f., 208
Lin Shui Nai 林水奶, 48, 51, 53 f., 57
Ling Kuan T'ien Chün 靈官天君
Liu Pang 劉邦, 164
Liu Pei 劉備, 165
Luh Ki 陸機 (261–303), commander and poet, 178
Lü Tung Pin 呂洞濱, 81 ff.
Lü Yen 呂喦, 82

Ma Tsu P'o 媽祖婆, 103 f., 108, 110 f.
Miao Chuang 妙莊, 71
Mien Shan 綿山, 88
Mu Lien 目連, 66
Mo 末, 60

Nan 南, 44

Pao Yüeh Kuang 寶月光, 28—precious moonlight
Ping wu 丙午, 29
Po-chi 伯奇, 209
Pu T'ing Hu Yü 不廷胡余, 103

P'u Ming Hsiang Yen Shan, Universal Brightness Incense Mountain 普明香炎山, 30

Sha Ch'i 煞氣, 21
Shang-szŭ 上巳, 100
Shangti 上帝, 4, 26, 94, 170, 227, 232 f.
Shang yüan 上元, 41
Shê 社, 58
Shê Chi 社稷, 60
Shê Huei 社會, 58
Shen 神, 34, 110
Shen, cyclical character, 申, 22, 23
Shen Chou 神洲, 147
Shen hai 申亥, 23
Shen Nung 神農, 94, 202
Shen T'u 神荼, 2
Sung Shan, in Hunan, 嵩山, 113
Szŭ 巳, 100 f.
Ta Shih Chih, a Bodhisattva belonging to the retinue of Amitabha, 大勢至, 73
Tao 道, 38, 81 f.
Ting 丁, 42
Ti 帝, 76, 117
Tou 斗, 78
Tsao 棗, 124
Tsu-men 俎門, 209
Tuan Gate 端門, 209
Tuan Yang 端陽, 126
T'ai Hao 太昊, 113
T'ai Shan 泰山, 27, 113 ff., 116, 117, 119 ff., 142, 212
T'ai Sui 太歲, 20 f., 22, 97

T'eng-chien 騰簡, 209
T'eng-ken 騰根, 209
T'ien Hou 天后, 109
T'ien Kung, lord of Heaven, 天公, 27, 32
Ts'ao O 曹娥 in Chinese Reader's Manual No. 764, 185 f.
Ts'ao Ts'ao 曹操, 166
Ts'o-tuan 錯斷, 209

Wang-liang 罔兩, 210
Wei-chiao 葦茭, 210
Wei-shê 委蛇, 211
Wei-sui 委隨, 209
Wen Ch'ang 文昌, 75 f., 77, 80 f.
Wenshu, Mandjusri, a Bodhisattva of Wu T'ai Shan in northern Shansi, 文殊, 68
Wu 巫, 101

Yama, in China one of the rulers in Hades, 閻羅, 72, 194
Yang, male, positive, force in nature, 陽, 22, 37, 39, 78, 81, 88, 92 f., 101, 123, 126 ff., 129, 148, 153, 155, 163, 185, 200 f., 205 f., 228
Yao Kuang 妖光, 155
Yen Ti 炎帝, 123 f.
Yin 陰, 37, 78, 81, 92, 101 f., 123 f., 126 f., 129, 133, 148, 153, 155 f., 163, 183, 185, 187, 200 f., 205 f., 228
Yu Yuan 有元, 18
Yü, jade, 玉, 26
Yü Ch'iang 禺疆, also called 禺京, 103
Yü Hsü 禺虢, 103
Yü Huang Shangti 玉皇上帝, 16, 26
Yü-Lei 鬱壘, 2, 210
Yü Ti 玉帝, 26
Yüeh Fei 岳飛, 174
Yüeh Lao 月老, 185
Yüeh Ling 月令, 206
Yüeh Ling Chang Chü 月令章句, 210

INDEX

Abandoned Souls, 161 f.
Abstaining from meat, 13
Abstinence, 172, 173, 222
Adonis, 31
Ahriman, 141
Altar of Heaven, 220 ff.
Amitabha, 70, 73
Analects, 76
Ancestors, 219 ; offering to, 7, 8
Ancestral tablets, 198
Apis, 31
Aquarius, 19, 207
Aquila, 175
Ashtoreth, 146
August Heaven, 146
Avalokitesvara, 68 f.

Balances, 140
Bat, 17
Black dragon, 144
Blessings of heaven, 2
Board of Rites, 168, 193, 221, 222, 225
Books of Later Han, 208
Book of Poetry, 44
Book of Records, 113
Bringing down the moon, 182 f.
Budd, Charles, 178
Buddha, 167, 203
Buddhism, 194
Buddhist Patriarchs, 167
Buddhists, 203
Bureau of Sacrificial offerings, 224 f.
Burma, 108
Burning up old lanterns, 5, 6

Calendar, 10
Cambodia, 108
Canton, 104, 106, 111
Cassia, 188 f.
Chang Heng, 183, 186
Chao Lieh Ti, 165
Charms, 127, 128
Chekiang, 106, 111, 165

Chihli, 176, 203
Chou, 102
Chou Li, 86, 87, 101, 154, 200, 206
Chou Ts'ang, 168
Christianity, 32
Chinese Republic, 112
City Guardian, 43, 193 ff.
Cleansing Processions, 205 ff.
Cock, 203
Cold food, feast of, 86 ff.
Confucianism, 164
Confucius, 102, 141, 168, 208, 212
Courage, 166
Court of Imperial Entertainment, 232
Court of Supreme Imperial Sacrifices, 221
Court of Sacrificial Worship, 222
Cycle, 23
Ch'ang O, 186
Ch'eng Huang, 193
Ch'ing K'ang-ching, 101, 146
Ch'ing Ming, 86, 89, 91, 92 f.
Ch'ü Yüan, 183

Dang Dong, 5, 6
Dragon, 139 ff.
Dragon Boat Festival, 126
Dragon boat races, 132 ff.
Dragon boats, 132 ff.
Dragon bones, 142 ; Lords, 137 ; saliva, 142 ; teeth, 142 ; writings, 142

Earth, 17, 66, 212, 219
Easter, 86
Eight Immortals, 82 ; Genii, 81 ; Spirits, 202
Eleusinian Mysteries, 31
Exorcist, 133 f.

Fans, 130
Fares doubled, 16
Fen Yin, 148

Ferris Wheel, 44
Filial Porridge, 66
Fire-crackers, 6
Fire, god of, 214 ff.
Five sacred mountains, 113, 149; guardian mountains, 149
Flowers of the Seasons, 198
Folkways, 1
Foochow, 20, 176, 179, 196, 198
Foochow City, 100, 106, 171
Four Seas, 147, 149
Frog in the Moon, 187
Fukien, 104, 106 f., 111, 164

Gambling, 16
God of the ground, 215 f.; of the hearth, 214 ff.; of Heaven, 216; of wealth, 17
Goddess of Mercy, 68; of the moon, 185
Grand Canal, 108
Great Bear, 179; Dipper, 78, 79; Tomb, 207; Year, 20, 97 ff.
Greetings on New Year, 16
Guardian God, 134 f.
Gunpowder, 6, 7

Hades, 34 ff., 48, 62, 117 ff., 159, 161
Han dynasty, 102, 103, 164 f., 192, 212
Han Shun Ti, 211
Hangchow, 189
Harvest Festival, 179 ff.
Heaven, 17, 18, 62, 66, 95, 179, 191, 194, 201, 212, 216 f., 219, 225, 231, 234 f.
Heaven and Earth, 11 f., 15
Heaven, offering to, 4, 5, 220 ff.
Heavenly Ruler, 17
Hermits, 81 f.
Hinghwa, 104
Honan, 104, 177
Hou Chi, 202
Hou T'u, 146
Hou T'u Ch'i, 146
Household Gods, 4
Huangti, 170 f.
Hunan, 6, 165

Hunters' festival, 203 f.
Hupeh, 165, 166, 171

Iliad, 146
Imperial Board of Astronomy, 223
India, 164
Indra, 167
Ishtar, 146
Isis, 31
Isles of the Immortals, 82

Jade Emperor, 26
Jen Tsung, 223
Jupiter, 97 ff.

Kalpas, 30
Kang Wu, 188
Kiangsi, 83
Kiangsu, 165
Kin Tartars, 106 f., 191
Kite flying, 190 ff.
Kou Mang, 20, 24
Kuan P'ing, 168
Kuan Ti, 48, 62
Kuan Tzu, 88, 113
Kuanyin, 42, 50, 62, 68 ff., 105
Kuan Yü, 164 ff.
Kublai, 107 f.
Kunlun, 147 ff.
Kwangtung, 6, 164
Kweichow, 13
K'ai Feng, 106
K'ai Ming Wang, 22
K'ou-t'ou, 200, 226, 230, 232, 233

Lake Baikal, 107
Lantern festival, 41 ff.
Lao Tzu, 28, 29, 141
Li Chi, 19, 20, 21, 94, 103, 155, 206, 208
Liao dynasty, 191
Liaotung, 164
Lin Fang, 212
Lin Shui Nai, 51 ff.
Literature, god of, 75
Liu Pang, 164
Liu Pei, 165
Loochoo Islands, 137
Lord of Heaven, 175

Loyalty, 166
Loyang, 165
Luh-ki, 178
Lü Tung Pin, 81
Lyra, 175

Mahayana, 68
Manchu dynasty, 193, 194
Man in the moon, 184 f.
Maras, 167
Materia Medica, 130
Ma Tsu P'o, 103 ff.
Mayers' Chinese Reader's Manual, 85
Medicine, 177
Medicines, 130, 131
Mencius, 48
Milky way, 175, 177
Ming dynasty, 109, 168, 193
Mirror in purgatory, 195
Mongol dynasty, 195
Mongols, 107 ff.
Moon, journeys to, 182
Mother Earth, 146 ff.
Mo Tzu, 191
Mottoes in houses, 1, 2
Müller, Max, 26
Musca Borealis, 207
Musicians, 224

Nanking, 107, 165
Nature assisted by magic, 15
Nestorian missionaries, 69
New Year, 18
New Year customs, 10 ff.

Old Buddha, 43
Osiris, 31

Palm Sunday, 90
Paper with characters, 197
Peach-tree, symbol of immortality, 2
Pearly Emperor, 26 ff.
Pegasus, 207
Peking, 106, 108, 148, 201, 220
Pleiades, 207
Posturers, 224, 232
Potala, 68

Prayer, 95, 115, 143 f., 150, 159f., 202, 228, 229
Prayer-tablet, 223 ff., 228, 232
Presents, 130, 199 f.
Preventing disease, 13, 14
Procession, 194 ff., 224
Prognostication of weather, 200 f.
Purgatory, 194, 195

Queen of the West, 82
Queen of the Western Paradise, 72

Rabbit in the moon, 183
Reunion at New Year, 7
Revolution, 145
Rites, Book of, 92, 123, 129
Rolls of silk, 224
Roman Empire, 164
Ruler of Earth, 158; of Heaven, 41, 159; of Water, 158

Sacrifice to Heaven, 220 ff.
Sakyamuni, 188, 203
Scorpio, 79, 140

T'aiping Rebellion, 168
T'ai Shan, 27, 113 ff., 212
T'ai Tsu, 223
T'ang, 103, 105, 208
T'ang dynasty, 167, 182
Ts'in dynasty, 168

Ursa Major, 75, 76, 207, 216

Vega, 175
Virgo, 140
Vishnu, 68
Vows, 196 f.

Wandering spirits, 7
Wang Ch'ung, 143, 183
Wang Mang, 146
Weather prognostications, 14 f., 181 f.
Weaver and the herdsman, 175 f.
Wei, 166
Wei dynasty, 165
Western Paradise, 82

Western Tsin, 165
White sparrow, 27
Wind, 15
Winter Solstice, 198 ff.
Wu dynasty, 165

Yama, 194
Yang, 100, 129, 148, 153, 155, 156, 163, 200 f., 205 f., 210 f., 211, 228, 232
Yangtze River, 104, 106, 210
Yao, 103, 193
Yih Ching, 187

Yimpu, 6
Yin, 100 f., 129, 148, 153, 155, 156, 163, 183, 187, 200 f., 205, 210 f., 228
Yuan dynasty, 193
Yuan Shih-kai, 173 f.
Yüeh Fei, 174
Yüeh Ling, 206 f., 212
Yü Ch'üan, 166
Yü Lei, 2
Yünnan, 13, 164
Yü Ti, 26
Yu Yuan, 18

PROBSTHAIN'S ORIENTAL SERIES.

PROBSTHAIN'S ORIENTAL SERIES.—VOL. I.
The Indian Craftsmen. By A. K. COOMARASWAMY. *Out of Print.*

PROBSTHAIN'S ORIENTAL SERIES.—VOL. II.
Buddhism as a Religion: Its Historical Development and its Present-Day Condition. By H. HACKMANN, Lic. Theol. 8vo, pp. 320. 1910.
Temporarily Out of Print.

Contents: Preface; I, The Buddha and His Doctrine; II, Sketch of the History of Buddhism; III, Southern Buddhism (Ceylon, Burma, Siam); IV, Lamaism; V, Eastern Buddhism (China, Korea, Japan); Conclusion, Bibliography; Index. The only complete work on Buddhism.

PROBSTHAIN'S ORIENTAL SERIES.—VOLS. III & IV.
The Masnavi. By JALALU'D-DIN RUMI, Book II, translated for the first time into English Prose by Professor C. E. Wilson. 2 vols: Vol. I, Translation from the Persian; Vol. II, Commentary. 8vo. 1910. Price 30s.

"Wilson's nüchterne fast wörtliche Uebersetzung in verein mit seinen Erlaüterungen lässt Keinen, aber auch Keinen Wunsch unbefriedigt."—*Der Islam*, Vol. II, p. 292.

"Wilson's translation of the Second Book of the Masnavi is an important addition to our knowledge of the greatest of all Sufi poets. The notes, though very full, are no more elaborate than the veiled sentences of the original require in order to make them intelligible to one who is not versed in the conventionalities of Persian and especially of Sufi diction. It is to be hoped that Wilson will translate the last four books of the poem in the same thorough way."—*American Journal of Theology*.

ARTHUR PROBSTHAIN, ORIENTAL PUBLISHER.

PROBSTHAIN'S ORIENTAL SERIES.—VOL. V.

Essays : Indian and Islamic. By S. Khuda Bukhsh, M.A., Oxon. 8vo, pp. 295. 1911. Price 8s. 6d.

". . . The Author has carried on his studies with scrupulous fidelity to science and truth. He is a faithful historian, and a historian of Islam unparalleled in this country, for having adopted the true critical method. Much has been brought to light to add to the sum total of historical experience . . ."—*Modern Review*, Calcutta.

PROBSTHAIN'S ORIENTAL SERIES.—VOL. VI.

Bactria : The History of a Forgotten Empire. By H. G. Rawlinson, M.A., I.E.S. 8vo, pp. xxiii, 168, with 2 maps. and 5 plates. 1912. Price 10s. 6d.

PROBSTHAIN'S ORIENTAL SERIES.—VOL. VII.

A Brief History of Early Chinese Philosophy. By Dr. T. Suzuki, Tokyo University. 8vo, pp. 200. 1914. Price 8s. 6d.

" The authorities on the philosophy or religion of the Chinese are so few that one offers a welcome at once to a scholarly Japanese who has made a real study of the subject. The title is too modest, and the work is all clear and competent."—*Expository Times*.

PROBSTHAIN'S ORIENTAL SERIES.—VOLS: VIII & IX.

The I-Li, or Book of Etiquette and Ceremonial. Translated from the Chinese, with Introduction, Notes, Illustrations, and Plans, by John Steele, M.A., D.Litt. Cr. 8vo. Two volumes. 1917. Price 30s.

" The issue of the I-Li in two volumes is an event of Sinology. The student of Chinese must ever be grateful to Dr. Steele for the production of this laborious work, which will be of great help to those who follow him."—*Journal of North China Branch, R.A.S.*

ARTHUR PROBSTHAIN, ORIENTAL PUBLISHER.

PROBSTHAIN'S ORIENTAL SERIES.—VOLS. X & XI.

The Philosophy of Human Nature (Hsing Li). By CHU HSI. Translated from the Chinese, with Notes, by J. Percy Bruce, M.A., D.Litt. 2 volumes.
Vol. I: Introduction, Chu Hsi and his Masters. Cr. 8vo, pp. xvi, 336. Price 24s.
Vol. II: Translation, The Philosophy of Human Nature. Cr. 8vo, pp. xvi, 444. Price 36s.

Chu Hsi (A.D. 1130–1200) is the most eminent amongst the later Chinese philosophers, and the great critic and expositor of the ethical writings of Confucius. A biography and commentary on the teachings and speculations of this most remarkable and authoritative commentator and thinker has become imperative. Chu Hsi's notes on the classics are accepted as orthodox, and they were, till recent change, printed with the text and committed to memory by all Chinese students.

From the foregoing note the value of the work will readily be acknowledged. Mr. Bruce, himself a great scholar, has accomplished his task in a unique manner and offers to the Chinese, to philosophers, and theologians, the fruit of his vast labours.

"Mr. Bruce's translation is the first serious and extensive attempt to introduce Sung Philosophy to Europe. His translation is careful and exact, and he has earned the gratitude of all who study the history of Chinese thought."—*Times* "Literary Supplement".

PROBSTHAIN'S ORIENTAL SERIES.—VOLS. XII & XIII.

Nizami: The Haft Paikar, or the Life of King Bahrām Gūr, and the seven stories told by his Seven Queens, translated from the Persian, with full commentary by Prof. C. E. WILSON, B.A. 2 vols. Cr. 8vo. 1924. Price 32s.

Throughout this work, the most attractive of Nizami's poems, lies an undercurrent of Sufism, which will interest students of mysticism. All linguistic difficulties have been solved by Professor Wilson in his commentary of over 2,000 notes, in which much historical and geographical information can also be found.

"The 'Oriental Series' inaugurated by Messrs. Probsthain and Co., deserves the patronage of Orientalists and students of Asiatic literature and philosophies. In it have been issued, so far, some excellent, original works and translations of great merit of Eastern classics. The latest addition to the series is Mr. C. E. Wilson's translation (from the Persian) of the *Haft Paikar* ('The Seven Beauties') of the famous mystic poet—Nizami of Ganja—enriched with an elucidative commentary. Nizami's *Haft Paikar* is a renowned classic in Persian poetry, and in the literature of mysticism it may be said to stand second only to the Masnavi of Jalalu-ud-din Rumi. An English translation of it, with an adequate commentary, was badly needed alike by the student of Persian literature and Oriental mysticism."—*Hindustan Review*.

ARTHUR PROBSTHAIN, ORIENTAL PUBLISHER.

PROBSTHAIN'S ORIENTAL SERIES.—VOL. XIV.

The World Conception of the Chinese: their Astronomical, Cosmological, and Physico-Philosophical Speculations. By Professor A. FORKE. Cr. 8vo, pp. xiv, 300. 1925. Price 24s.

"This is the first attempt at a systematic digest of Chinese Natural Philosophy based on original sources. The Chinese mind cannot be understood unless we know its ideas on the Cosmos and the Cosmological Agencies with which the moral forces are intimately connected."

It is an invaluable reference book. Every Library interested in promoting understanding about the Origins of Chinese ideas should have a copy.—*Chinese Recorder*.

PROBSTHAIN'S ORIENTAL SERIES.—VOLS. XV & XVI.

Hsüntze. By HOMER H. DUBS. 2 volumes. Vol. I: The Moulder of Ancient Confucianism. Cr. 8vo, pp. x, 304. 1927. Price 24s.

Vol. II: Works: Translated from the Chinese. Cr. 8vo, pp. 336. 1927. Price 24s.

"The First European treatise of this great Philosopher, with full bibliography and fine index.

Hsüntze was a younger contemporary of Mencius, and, like Mencius, a defender of the Confucian faith. Hsüntze for the first time gave an orderly exposition of the Confucian Philosophy; as a result it was his form of teaching which was most influential upon succeeding generations of Chinese. Because of a misunderstanding of his doctrine that human nature is evil, his writings were not made part of the Confucian canon, but he has always been regarded as the most important of non-canonical writers, and they have always formed part of the study of every educated Chinese.

"This volume is a magnificent contribution to that series of interpretations and descriptions of Chinese thinkers and thought which means so much to the setting up of mutual appreciation and understanding between the East and the West. We are glad to have this excellent portrait of the mind of Hsüntze, even though we must admit we are not greatly thrilled over his authoritarian ethics."—*Chinese Recorder*.

ARTHUR PROBSTHAIN, ORIENTAL PUBLISHER.

PROBSTHAIN'S ORIENTAL SERIES.—VOL. XVII.

The Book of Lord Shang. A Classic of the Chinese School of Law. Translated from the Chinese with Introduction and Notes, by J. J. L. DUYVENDAK (University of Leyden). Cr. 8vo, pp. 350. 1929.
Price 24s.
Chinese Editions of "The Book of Lord Shang" are available.

Lord Shang (Shang Yang, or Wei Yang) taught that Law, not morality, was the chief factor in ruling a state. Of recent years there has been a great deal of interest in China in this school of thought, because the chief problem which confronts her is that of replacing the old Confucian system of government, with its moral idealism, by the modern conception of a state ruled by Law. Shang Yang himself as a statesman laid the foundation of the later greatness of the country of Ch'in.

This translation incorporates the results of recent Chinese research; numerous footnotes and references give the necessary explanations, and in a lengthy introduction a critical study is given of the man, the book, and the school of thought to which it belongs.

PROBSTHAIN'S ORIENTAL SERIES.—VOL. XVIII.

Folkways in China. By PROFESSOR LEWIS HODOUS (Hartford Seminary Foundation), Hartford, Conn. Ready Shortly. Price ~~about 20s.~~ 12/6

This volume is the result of personal observation during a long residence in China. While much of the work was done at Foochow, other parts of China made substantial contributions. Some of the stories were collected on a 200 mile walk through Shansi, Hunan, and Hupeh.

The illustrations were selected from a large number collected during several years, and are unique.

It is hoped that this work will make a contribution to the understanding of the Chinese who live and toil on the soil.

PROBSTHAIN'S ORIENTAL SERIES.—VOLS. XIX & XX.

Ready Shortly.

Motse: Works Ethical and Political. Translated from the Chinese. By Y. P. MEI. 16/-

Motse: His Life and Times. By Y. P. MEI. To be published in conjunction with the Translation of the Works.

It should be pointed out that these two volumes will appear at a most opportune time, and that the teachings of this great philosopher should be closely studied by present-day statesmen and politicians.

ARTHUR PROBSTHAIN, ORIENTAL PUBLISHER.

PROBSTHAIN'S ORIENTAL PUBLICATIONS

Probsthain (Arthur). Encyclopaedia of Books on China. Containing 4,624 titles of works (European and Chinese). 1928. 30s.

Vogel (Prof. J. Ph.). Indian Serpent-Lore, or the Nagas in Hindu Legend and Art. Cr. 4to, pp. 318, with 30 plates. 1927. 42s.

Baker (D. C.). T'ai Shan: An Account of the Sacred Eastern Peak of China. 8vo, pp. xx, 225. 1925. 12s.

Brunnert (H. S.) and **Hagelstrom** (V. V.). Present Day Political Organization of China. Roy. 8vo, pp. lxxx, 572. 1912. £3 3s.

Bryan (R. T.) An Outline of Chinese Civil Law. 8vo, pp. vi, 92. 1925. 8s.

Catalogue of an Exhibition of Chinese Applied Art: Bronzes, Pottery, Porcelain, Jades, Embroideries, Carpets, Enamels, Lacquers, etc., held in the Manchester Art Galley, 1913, with Introduction by Wm. Burton. 4to, pp. 104, with 17 plates. 1913. 12s. 6d.

Cornaby (W.). A Necklace of Peachstones. "A String of Chinese Peachstones," re-written with Appendix of Chinese Lighter Literature. 8vo, pp. 421. 1925. 18s.

Fitkin (G. M.). The Great River: the Story of a Voyage on the Yangtze Kiang. Roy. 8vo, pp. v, 153, and 28 illustrations. 1922. 18s.

Fletcher (W. J. B.). Gems of Chinese Verse, translated into English Verse. Roy. 8vo, pp. 249. 1919. 8s.

Fletcher (W. J. B.). More Gems of Poetry. Chinese Text, with English Translation and Notes. Roy. 8vo, pp. 208. Second edition, 1923. 8s.

Hirth (F.). Native Sources for the History of Chinese Pictorial Art. English Version by A. E. Meyer. With Index of artists, authors, and books. 8vo, pp. 28. 1917. 3s. 6d.

Hirth Anniversary Volume, presented to Friedrich Hirth, Professor of Chinese, Columbia University, New York, in Honour of his Seventy-fifth Birthday, by his friends and admirers. 1923. £3 15s.

The work contains 28 original and scholarly contributions dealing with the Professor's particular specialities, and will ever be a work of the first order of Chinese and Central Asian Studies.

Hosie (A.). On the trail of the Opium Poppy: a Narrative of Travel in the Chief Opium Producing Provinces of China. 2 volumes, 8vo, with plates and maps. 1914. 25s.

The work records the observations of an Oriental traveller of wide experience upon the places, people, products, industries and trades.

Hu Shih. The Development of Logical Method in Ancient China. pp. 187. 1922. 7s. 6d.

Johnson (O. S.). A Study of Chinese Alchemy. 8vo, pp. xiv, 156. 1928. 12s.

Kacyapaparivarta: A Mahayanasutra of the Ratnakuta Class, edited in the original Sanskrit, in Tibetan and in Chinese, by A. von Staël-Holstein. Volume I. Large 8vo, pp. xxvi, 232. 1926. £1 4s.

The Chinese is in Chinese Characters, the Tibetan and the Sanskrit in Roman characters only.

ARTHUR PROBSTHAIN, ORIENTAL PUBLISHERS.

Kliene (C.). Anglo-Chinese Calendar for 250 Years (1751–2000). 4to, half calf. 1906. £2 10s.
This is the only large work of the kind, giving the comparative English and Chinese dates for 250 years. It is indispensable to every student of Chinese history.

Kotenev (A. M.). Shanghai : Its Mixed Court and Council, Material relating to the History of the Shanghai Municipal Council and the History, Practice, and Statistics of the International Mixed Court, Chinese Modern Law and Shanghai Municipal Land Regulations and Bye-Laws governing the Life in the Settlement. Roy. 8vo, pp. 26, 588. 1925. 42s.

Kotenev (A. M.). Shanghai : Its Municipality and the Chinese : being the History of the Shanghai Municipal Council and its relations with the Chinese, the Practice of the International Mixed Court, and the Inauguration and Constitution of the Shanghai Provisional Court, Roy. 8vo, pp. xvi, 548. 1927. 36s.
A companion volume to " Shanghai, its Mixed Court and Council ".

Lanning (G.). Old Forces in New China : An Effort to Exhibit the Fundamental Relationship in China and the West in their True Light. 8vo, pp. x, 400, with a map showing the natural resources of China. 1912. 12s. 6d.

Li Ung Bing. Outlines of Chinese History. New Edition in preparation.

Macgowan (J.). Imperial History of China : History of the Empire as compiled by the Chinese Historians. Second edition, 8vo, pp. xi, 651, half calf. 1906. £1 10s.

McNair (H. F.). The Chinese Abroad, their Position and Protection. A Study in International Law and Relations. 8vo, pp. xxii, 340. 1925. 12s.

McNair (H. F.). Modern Chinese History. Selected Readings. A collection of extracts from various sources chosen to illustrate some of the chief phases of China's International Relations during the past hundred years. Second edition, 8vo, pp. xxxvii, 922. 1927. £1 12s.

McNair (H. F.). China's International Relations and Other Essays. 8vo, pp. vii, 326. 1926. 10s.

Mayers (W. R.). The Chinese Reader's Manual : A Handbook of Biographical, Historical, Mythological, and General Literary Reference. 8vo, pp. xvi, 444. 1924. £1 10s.

Morse (H. B.) and **McNair** (H. F.). Far Eastern International Relations. A comprehensive work presenting to the student and general reader a survey of incidents and conditions in the relations of the nations of the Far East with each other and the nations of the West. Roy. 8vo, pp. xv, 1128, with maps and illustrations. 1928. 32s.

Otte (F.). Translations from Modern Chinese. Chinese Text with English Translation. Fourth edition, revised, two volumes, 8vo. 1926. 7s.

Owen (Prof. G.). The Evolution of Chinese Writing. 8vo, pp. 32. 3s. 6d.

Parker (E. H.). Ancient China Simplified. 8vo, pp. xxxi, 232, with 9 maps of Ancient China and other plates. 1908. 12s. 6d.
A history of Civilization from the earliest times down to, and including, Confucius and Lao Tze.

ARTHUR PROBSTHAIN, ORIENTAL PUBLISHERS.

Perlmann (S. M.). Hassinim (the Chinese), Chinese Life, Manners, and Customs, Culture and Creeds, Government System and Trade, with an Appendix, the Jews in China, in Hebrew. 8vo, 1911. 4s.

Playfair (G. M. H.). The Cities and Towns of China : A Geographical Dictionary, Second Edition, large 8vo, pp. 89, 582. 1910. 32s.

Plopper (C. H.). Chinese Religion seen through the Proverb. Vol. I. 8vo, pp. ix, 381. 1926. 21s.
Treatises on the Chinese Religion, with Proverbs pertaining thereto in Chinese, with English translation and Notes. The subjects are: Survivals of Ancient Nature Worship; Heaven Animism; Magic Buddahood; the Pantheon ;Temple Life ; Religious Doctrines; Rewards and Punishments; Fate; Life Beyond the Grave; Bibliography; Index of Authors quoted; Index.

Price (M. T.). Christian Missions and Oriental Civilizations, a Study in Culture Contact ; the Re-actions of Non-christian Peoples to Protestant Missions from the Standpoint of Individual and Group Behaviour, Outline, Materials, Problems, and Tentative Interpretations. 8vo, pp. xxvi, 578. 1924. 16s.

Rasmussen (O. D.). What's Right With China ? 8vo, pp. xx, 255. 1927. 14s.

Reichelt (K. L.). Truth and Tradition in Chinese Buddhism. A Study of Chinese Mahayana Buddhism, translated from the Norwegian. 8vo, pp. xiii, 330, illustrated. 1927. 12s.

Remer (C. F.). The Foreign Trade of China. 8vo, pp. xii, 269. 1926. 16s.

Remer (C. F.). Readings in Economics for China, Selected Materials. with explanatory introductions. 8vo, pp. x, 685. 1926. £1 1s.

Richard (L.). Comprehensive Geography of the Chinese Empire. 8vo, with maps. 1901. 21s.

Scarborough (W.). A Collection of Chinese Proverbs, revised and enlarged by 600 Proverbs by C. W. Allan. Chinese Text in Chinese and Roman characters, with English Translation. 8vo, pp. vi, 381, 14. 1927. 24s.

Sun Yat Sen. San Min Chu I : The Three Principles of the People, translated from the Chinese by F. W. Price. 8vo, pp. xvii, 514. 1927. Cloth 16s. 1928. Paper 8s.

Vitale (Baron G.). Chinese Folklore : Pekinese Rhymes, first collected and edited, with Notes and English Translation. 8vo, pp. xvii, 220. 1896. 16s.

Vitale (Baron G.). Chinese Merry Tales, collected and edited in Chinese ; a First Reading Book for Students of Colloquial Chinese, Second edition, 8vo, pp. viii, 118. 1908. 10s.

Willoughby (W. W.). Foreign Rights and Interests in China. Second edition, 2 vols, roy. 8vo, 1927. £2 15s.

Wu (Kuo-Cheng). Ancient Chinese Political Theories. 8vo, pp. 340. 1928. 16s.
The author gives a definite and systematic expression to the unascertained and detached political conceptions in ancient China.

Wylie (A.). Notes on Chinese Literature (reprint). Roy. 8vo, pp. 40, 307. 1923. 18s.

ARTHUR PROBSTHAIN, ORIENTAL PUBLISHERS.